Preach Your Best Sermon Ever

*Other Books by
King Duncan*

King's Treasury of Dynamic Preaching

The Great and Not So Great Love Stories of the Bible

The Amazing Law of Influence

The One-Minute Motivator

Amusing Grace: Humor to Heal Mind, Soul, and Body

I Love You, Dad

Help! I've Fallen Down Laughing . . . and Can't Get Up

Preach Your Best Sermon Ever

Preaching Sermons that Excite and Energize!

King Duncan
Dynamic Preaching

Copyright 2014 by King Duncan
No part of this book may be reproduced in any manner whatsoever without the express written permission of the copyright holder.

Published by
Seven Worlds Publishing

Unless otherwise noted, all scriptures are from the New International Version (NIV) Copyright (c) 1973, 1978, 1984 by International Bible Society.

Contents

Introduction	7
The Rachel Principle	11
The Most Important Truth about Preaching	17
Where Meaning Occurs	23
Preaching to the Whole Brain	25
Tell Me a Story!	33
The Story is the Sermon	41
The Hero's Adventure	45
When You Need to Be Prophetic	51
About Narrative Preaching	55
Telling the Biblical Story	67
The Art of Sermon Illustration	71
Four Levels of Illustrations	87
Finding Exciting Sermon Illustrations	93
Add Drama to Your Preaching	107
More Tips for Elevating Your Preaching	129
Using Humor in the Pulpit	157
Postscript	177
Shifting Paradigms for Ministry in the 21st Century	179
Notes	181
References	185

*In Memory of the Rev. Jerry Anderson and
the Rev. Ray Robinson*
Dear Friends and Devoted Pastors

*Special thanks to Angela Akers
As always for her invaluable assistance*

Introduction

One of my favorite preacher/writers Bruce Larson tells about a cartoon that was published in *The New Yorker* magazine some years ago. Two men are standing on a street corner across from a church. It is Sunday noon and people are pouring out of the church, cheering, laughing, arms in the air, some dancing. In the middle of all this, they are carrying out their pastor on their shoulders. Observing this, one man says to the other, "I wonder what he preached on?"

Bruce Larson says, "I suspect this cartoon stays with me because I would like to be a preacher who could turn people on like that. I would like to be one of the worshipers under a preacher like that. I would like the church itself to be a place where such genuine feelings can be released." [1]

So do I, Bruce. I have to say there are few things that irk me more than dull, lifeless preaching. I yawn when I hear dull preaching, then I get angry. How dare that pastor waste my time! Even more importantly, how dare that pastor take the greatest privilege given to any man or woman, the privilege of standing before God's people and proclaiming God's Word, and waste it by being boring!

Now, you may think there aren't any dull preachers—and I know that it doesn't apply to you—but I sit out in the congregation most Sundays and let me tell you, there is some dull preaching going on!

I can sympathize with one seminary professor who said that there are three kinds of student sermons: dull, duller and inconceivably dull. I've heard some of those inconceivably dull sermons.

One Methodist bishop said that one of his preachers is supernaturally dull: "Nobody could be that dull without divine help." I've also heard some of those supernaturally dull sermons, and it is tragic.

A child tugs at her mother's sleeve during the worship service. "Mommy," she asks, "are you sure this is the only way to get to heaven?"

Fred Craddock tells of the pastor who was watching cars go around the track at the Indy 500. At first it's exciting, the great crowd and the noise. But pretty soon, he becomes bored. Secretly, he hopes for a crash just to have some excitement.

Craddock asks, "Have you ever secretly cheered when a child fell out of a pew or a bird flew in a window or the sound system picked up a police call or a dog came down the aisle and curled up to sleep under the pulpit?" [2]

He compares a congregation enduring dull preaching to passengers on a cruise ship who begin to ask one another hopefully, "Do you think it will storm?"

I guess it's been true in every generation. Charles Spurgeon once said, "Some ministers would make good martyrs; they are so dry they would burn well." That's sad. Nothing will kill the spiritual life of people like dull, colorless, passionless preaching. Sydney Smith once said that blasphemy against the Holy Spirit in the pulpit is dullness. I agree.

And here is why I get so upset when I think about this subject. *There is no excuse for dryness in the pulpit.* Any pastor of at least moderate intelligence can be an effective, exciting preacher by following a few simple rules.

That's what this book is about. It's a transcript taken from hundreds of workshops I have led for pastors of almost every theological tradition on communicating the Gospel in an image-driven world. I thought about presenting these ideas in a more formal style. But I was afraid that my passion might not come through. Besides, I wanted this book to resemble what I look for in a sermon. Short sentences, short paragraphs, and a limited vocabulary so that it might be accessible to a broad audience. Unfortunately, because this

Introduction

material was presented with only a minimum of notes over a period of several years, it has been impossible to trace many of the sources. I have credited those I could find. I apologize for those I could not.

So here are some unfiltered, but time-tested, keys to communicating the Gospel from the pulpit in an exciting and energizing way. I trust you will find them both constructive and helpful.

The Rachel Principle

One Sunday about noon, I held my six-year-old granddaughter's hand as we walked toward the car after church. It was the first time she had attended a worship service with us. I asked her what she thought of the pastor. "He could use more color," she replied matter-of-factly.

"What do you mean, Rachel?" I asked. I was intrigued.

"He's not very exciting," she replied. "You know," she said thoughtfully, "It's important to make the things that are true exciting, because the things that aren't true are always exciting."

Whoa! Out of the mouths of babes. *It's important to make the things that are true exciting . . .*

That was many years ago. We've moved. We have a different pastor now. But the principle has not changed. What are you doing to add excitement to your preaching?

Now, to some pastors, this is not an important question. They see themselves primarily as those who maintain the church's traditions. Their call, as they see it, is to faithfully expound the Word. The effect of their preaching on their listeners is God's business, not theirs. If you are in that company, you need read no further.

If, on the other hand, you believe that the effect your preaching has on your congregation is at least partially in your hands, and if you long to preach so that lives are changed and the community of faith increased with the result that the Kingdom of God comes alive in your community, then keep reading.

Chances are many of the things you learned about preaching in seminary are now obsolete. Does that surprise you? Why? The rapid changes brought about by technology in our society in nearly every sector are astounding. Why should these changes not affect preaching?

Obviously, I believe they do. I'm going to deal to some extent with some of these changes and why they are demanding a new approach to homiletics. But first, I want to give you another principle that will be crucial to our discussion: *few people will remember what you say in your message; what they will remember is how they felt while you were saying it.* Were they bored, confused, depressed, angry? Or were they excited, energized, convicted, inspired? Did they want to carry you out of church on their shoulders, or did they resent you waking them from a pleasant, twenty-minute snooze?

There is still a place for preaching in this high tech, high touch world. Texas pastor Bill Hinson tells about preaching in a suburban church in Houston. He was startled as he walked toward the pulpit to see a fire extinguisher attached to the side of the pulpit. It was the only fire extinguisher that he saw anyplace in that church. At first, he thought such a site selection strange. Upon reflection, however, he believes the fire extinguisher was carefully placed. "If and when," he comments, "a great fire begins to burn in our churches, it will have begun in the pulpits. If it does not start there, the people in the pews will never have their own hearts set ablaze." [3]

Amen to that. There are many who say that preaching has no place in a postmodern world. For one thing, there is a decided resistance to authority figures. Even scientists are under a skeptical microscope nowadays. John Sweetman writes, "Postmodernists react against the expert. They are thoroughly skeptical of people who stand in ivory towers and espouse their views. According to the postmodernists, unquestioned, self-appointed experts have only created legalism, division and intolerance. They believe that truth for a community is much better discerned in community . . ." [4]

I have been working this past year in a church that is aimed squarely at postmoderns, and my experience is that Sweetman is on target. The entire attitude toward authority has radically changed. As for formal presentations—even those enhanced by visual aids such as PowerPoint® and short video clips—they are increasingly ineffective in a world where communications are rapidly becoming more.

I have been impressed by Mark Miller's work, *Experiential Storytelling*. He says, "Radio, television, computers, and finally the Internet created an entirely new world. Old techniques were increasingly met with a 'been there, done that' attitude. People want interaction, something that will jar them out of their monotony. They want to be touched, not by the numbing effect of a top-down monologue aimed at the mind, but by the power of a full-bodied personal experience." Miller calls for worship and preaching to be more experiential. [5]

I, too, in working with postmoderns have noticed how they respond to images, art, drama, dance, etc. The goal is to totally immerse the person in the pew in an experience of worship, not simply convey intellectual content. Nevertheless, I predict that the spoken word will still be at the heart of the worship experience for many years to come. For one thing, the spoken word is still a powerful medium. I like what Kyle Hazelton said, "Anyone who generalizes that a picture is worth a thousand words has never tried to capture John 3:16 in a picture." John 3:16 is only 25 words.

Emil Ludwig said of Napoleon in the Italian campaign, "Half of what he achieves is achieved by the power of words." Napoleon moved his soldiers to sacrifice everything they had to pursue his ambitions. Words are powerful. Hitler's rhetoric plunged the world into World War II and millions died; Churchill's words stirred millions to resist the aggression of *Der Fuehrer* and Hitler was defeated.

Following the war, the Russians built an Iron Curtain in Europe symbolized by the Berlin Wall. In June 1961, John F. Kennedy stood in front of the West Berlin City Hall and declared to the throng massed there, "Ich bin ein Berliner." He was letting the people of Berlin know that they were not alone in their struggle. And in 1987, President Ronald Reagan stood in front of the Berlin Wall and challenged Soviet Union leader Mikhail Gorbachev to "Tear down this wall!" On a visit to Europe this past year, my wife, Selina, and I stood in front of a fragment of that wall in awe of all that has transpired in our lifetime. And much of it is related to the power of speech.

The words of Abraham Lincoln have turned out to be more ironic than prophetic. Remember that in his Gettysburg address, he said, "The world will little note nor long remember what we say here; but it can never forget what they did here." In fact, millions of people are more familiar with Lincoln's words than they are with the battle of Gettysburg.

Regardless of your politics, it's no accident that the most popular president in recent times was known as The Great Communicator. Words matter. Words carry power. You may be a member of a denomination that was founded and fueled by men and women who understood the power of the spoken word. Imagine, you have that same privilege they had of having a group of people gather once a week for an hour or so to give you the opportunity to speak to them about whatever the Lord lays on your heart. That's powerful.

Preaching stands at the intersection of humanity's need and God's provision. The Latin word for priest is *pontifex*, which means bridge builder. And that is who you are when you mount the pulpit each Lord's Day. You are a bridge builder between a world in need and the One who can supply those needs.

John Killinger uses the analogy of people waiting on a dock in the days before mass communication. "This is their only contact with the world beyond the waters. They're waiting as the ship is tied to the moorings. They're waiting on news from the other side." [6]

Notice I said news and not views. They have not come to hear a theologian or a philosopher or a social analyst. They have come to hear their pastor—a man or a woman whom they believe walks with God and can tell them some news from God. The most important thing to remember is that those folks who gather on the Lord's Day need good news just as surely as did their parents or grandparents or a host of generations before them.

Most importantly, your congregation looks forward each week for a word from their pastor. To the average lay person, this is the most important item on the pastor's job description. They want you to preach the Gospel. If you are a pastor of a church of any size, the only time your people are exposed to you on a regular basis is when you are in the pulpit. If you do not minister to them there, then where? You can't make 500 pastoral calls per week.

I read about an exchange between two lay persons. One said, "Our minister's sermons aren't very good. But I forgive him that because during a recent crisis in our family, he was immensely attentive and helpful."

The other responded, "I'm afraid I can't overlook my pastor's homiletical shortcomings. My family has not needed his help in a crisis, and those sermons are the only pastoral care I get." [7]

Every once in a while, a pastor says to me, "King, you know preaching is really not my main interest. I'm basically a pastoral counselor." Well and good, but may I suggest that most of the pastoral counseling you'll do in your parish will be from the pulpit? That is, unless you can make two- or three-hundred calls a week or see two- or three-hundred people in your study, most of the pastoral help that you will give to your people will be from the pulpit.

Paul Shearer once observed that if the church were to die, the dagger in the heart would be the sermon. Preaching will be with us as long as the church exists. It is our approach to preaching that needs to change. My guess is that you recognize this. So, let's move on.

The Most Important Truth about Preaching

Preaching is an oral event. That is the most important truth about preaching. You say, "Well, King, that's obvious! Everybody knows that preaching is an oral event!" Well, do they? I've heard many pastors who seem to have no concept that preaching is an oral event.

One Sunday morning in a major city, I flicked on the television and caught a young priest presenting a homily. It was a well prepared message, very logical and very well-thought-out. He even used a joke! I know it was a joke because I had used it in one of the three joke books I had compiled. If I had not known beforehand that it was a joke, however, I would never have caught on. Why? Because the priest read through his message in a monotone voice with no pauses for emphasis, no attempt at eye contact, absolutely no recognition that there were human beings on the other end of the line who were depending on a very inefficient receiving system: a set of ears to translate and encode the priest's message into something meaningful for their lives.

Martin Luther once said that the church is a mouth house, not a pen house. That is, preaching is for ears, not for eyes. Communications guru Marshall McLuhan once contrasted reading and oral communication. McLuhan called reading a hot medium and speaking, or preaching, a cool medium.

The difference is that in reading, only one person is involved, the reader, and if the reader comes to something that he or she doesn't understand, then the reader can go back and read it again . . . or consult a dictionary or "google" it on a computer.

In an oral situation, however, the listener has only one chance to get what is said. And what's said must make an immediate impact—until, of course, that day comes when they put instant replay monitors in pews. At that point, we won't have to ask, "Now what did he or she say?" We'll simply hit a button, punch replay, and see the confusing section or sentence again. Of course, in the meantime, the preacher will have gone on to make another point which we will have missed. Then we will have to do another replay.

In oral communication, two people are involved: the preacher and the person in the pew, and the burden . . . note this . . . *the burden is on the preacher to keep the person in the pew involved.* That's the difference between preaching for eyes and preaching for ears. That's the difference between a mouth house and a pen house.

To make things more complicated, the worshipper is not a passive listener. In outmoded models of communication, there was an assumption that the person in the pew was sitting there like a sponge, just waiting to soak up all of the preacher's knowledge. If that's your assumption, you're in for a surprise. The listener in the pew is more like a rock than a sponge. If he or she soaks up anything, you've done a remarkable job.

There are many things going on in the listener's mind competing for his or her attention. Some of this competition is external. We're bombarded daily with thousands of messages, both visual and aural. If the preacher is not conscious of these competing messages, he or she will proceed to bombard folks as well. The result is that the message will be like water off the proverbial duck's back. The listener may sit there with a placid expression, but his or her mind may be a thousand miles away.

There may be a woman in the congregation who's been to the doctor that week. She's discovered a lump. Now this woman is waiting anxiously on the results of a biopsy. That distressing piece of information is coloring everything she hears. There may be a businessman, middle-aged, worried about losing his job. That's all he can think about. There may be a teenager who's having issues at school. Everything that happens in worship is filtered through that concern. Much is going on in the mind of your listener. Some of it may seem downright silly.

Maybe as you were entering the sanctuary Sunday morning you passed by Deacon Dave. You had your sermon on your mind or somebody else needed your attention, and you didn't speak to Deacon Dave. You didn't even see him. But Deacon Dave is sitting out there fuming, wondering why the pastor ignored him.

I spoke at a large, rural church one time and an elderly lady came up to me afterwards and said, "King, I've got a problem. You know our pastor is a wonderful young pastor."

I said, "Yes, he's terrific!" And he really was.

She said, "Have you noticed he's grown a moustache?"

If this pastor had come to this church at the very beginning with a moustache, it wouldn't have been a problem. But he had grown that moustache after this woman had gotten used to his naked face. She said, "King, I can't look at him while he's in the pulpit. I have to look out the window the whole time he's preaching."

Of course that's absurd. Freud would have loved having this lady as a patient. But, friend, it happens!

A man shook hands with his pastor following the service. "That was a great sermon, pastor!" he said, "You interrupted my thoughts several times!" An honest statement if I've ever heard one.

Listeners exercise selectivity. They exercise selectivity about what they are exposed to. There are some people who chose to stay away from your church last Sunday. Oh, maybe that doesn't happen in your church. Maybe you have 100% participation. In most churches, however, at least one member of the congregation chooses not to be in church. Now, maybe, just maybe, it has something to do with what happens in church.

I counseled with a woman one time who had fouled up her life royally. And her feeling was that she had better not go back to her church until she got her life completely in order. Friend, if this particular woman waits until she gets her life completely in order, it's going to be a long time before she's back in church.

Her pastor is a fine gentleman, but he's a rather moralistic, judgmental preacher. He has no idea that his preaching is standing as an obstacle to this woman coming back to church, rather than as an invitation to hear the good news of Jesus Christ. I meet many people who have been hurt by the church and for some, their pastor's sermons are an obstacle to their participation in worship.

Listeners exercise selectivity even when they come to worship. Again, don't assume because they are sitting in a pew with a placid expression on their face that they are actually listening. Maybe so, maybe not.

There was once a young man who attended a church that broadcast its worship service on the radio. The young man asked his pastor if could can wear a headset in worship and listen to the broadcast while the pastor was preaching.

The pastor, being a very affable person, said that would be fine. So, the young man sat there on Sunday morning with that headset on. The pastor said everything was fine until about half way through the sermon. It was then he noticed the young man patting his foot. The pastor knew he had changed channels.

Don't assume that just because people don't have a headset on, they don't change channels from time to time. In fact, many times during your message, they will do exactly that.

I have to confess that as a listener—somewhere in the middle of every sermon—my mind will wander off. I don't mean for that to happen, but I'm a sinner. My mind will often end up out in space somewhere—and then my pastor will say something like, "That reminds me of something that happened to me this week . . ." and that is an oral cue for me to get involved again in his message. If he doesn't give me those cues from time to time, my mind is going to stay out there in Never, Never Land.

Listeners not only exercise selectivity about what they listen to, they also exercise selectivity about what they really hear. Don't assume that what you said is what they heard.

A pastor said to me, "King, last Sunday I was preaching on grace, and I said very explicitly—in fact, I spent the entire sermon saying it—that no matter how hard we work at it, we can never work ourselves into the kingdom of God. So help me, a woman came up to me after that service and said, 'Oh, pastor, I'm so glad to hear you say that! I've always believed that if we just work hard enough, God will accept us!'" How does that happen?

When Bishop Willimon was a pastor, he had a mother call him and say, "Pastor, can you come over to talk to my daughter? She's been acting strange ever since she went to college. Now she has joined the Moonies!"

Willimon rushed over immediately to try to help the young girl see that she was mistaken in her new-found beliefs. "What on earth convinced you to get involved with these folks?" he asked.

She said that she had met a couple one evening who had taken her to a movie featuring the Rev. Moon. "When I heard him preach that night, I thought that I hadn't heard such good preaching since the last time I listened to you! That's why I'm a follower today. I owe it all to your preaching!"

It was at this point that Willimon remembered a conversation he had with an older and much more seasoned pastor. When he asked what the older man had learned in forty years of preaching, the older man replied, "What I have learned in preaching is that the possibilities for being misunderstood are virtually unlimited." [8]

Where Meaning Occurs

I want you to visualize for a moment a red piece of cloth. Imagine that you wave this red cloth in the face of an angry bull. What will happen? The bull may charge. Why? The time-honored myth is that bulls are excited by the color red. Probably that's not true. Bulls probably see only shades of grey, like most of the animal kingdom. I don't know anybody who's asked a bull directly, "Does the color red excite you?" but we believe that the bull is not responding to the color red, but to the movement of the cloth.

Why is this important? Stay with me. The color red is not so much the property of the cloth as it is a property of the human eye and brain. Our eye and our brain are so constructed that when light reflects off of an object, it absorbs some of the light and reflects the rest of it. Which wavelengths are reflected and which are absorbed depends on the properties of the object, but the interpretation of those wavelengths depends entirely on the photoreceptors in our eye and brain. We see color. But that happens in that wonderful organ we call an eye and in that unbelievably complex box we call a brain. A creature with a different set of eyes and a different brain would only see gray.

I often think that this is one of the proofs of the existence of God. Why would blind evolution give us this wonderful gift of being able to see color? It's not essential to our survival. But God has given us the wonderful gift of being able to see reds, and purples, and blues, etc.

Let's use another example. I cut my finger; it's bleeding profusely. I put disinfectant on it and a Band-Aid, and soon my finger heals. How does this occur? The healing is not in the disinfectant or the Band-Aid, is it? The disinfectant simply keeps the wound clean while the Band-Aid controls the bleeding. Meanwhile, the body does its healing thing. The healing comes from within.

In the same way, the meaning of a message resides in the listener, not in the message. That is, people come into your sanctuary with a preexisting set of images, pictures, symbols—all kinds of emotional anchors. They have a certain mindset, a world view, a set of paradigms, if you will. When you deliver your message, all you can hope is to somehow match your images, symbols, concepts and world view with their symbols, images, concepts and world view—and pray that meaning takes place. You don't give them meaning. The meaning comes from within, depending on their experiences.

I was talking with a communications expert who works with business speakers. He is a devoted member of his church. He said to me, "King, there are some fine preachers around."

I said, "Yes, there are."

He said, "But you know the thing that concerns me is how little effect preaching is having on lay people nowadays." He's right. We seem to be better at exposition of the Word than we are at evoking a meaningful response in the mind of the listener.

There is a story about a lady who was going door to door collecting for the Salvation Army. She went up to one household and rang the doorbell. A grumpy-looking man came to the door. She said, "Would you please donate to the Salvation Army?"

"I'm not interested," he said.

She said, "Don't you want to keep precious souls from going to hell?"

The man said, "Hummph, not enough folks are going to hell right now to suit me."

Okay, you've got one person in the congregation with that mindset, not enough people go to hell already; you've got another dear person who thinks everybody's going to go to heaven. Can you see that they're listening through two different sets of ears with two different sets of meaning? How do you bridge this gap?

Preaching to the Whole Brain

The average attention span today is . . . are you with me? The average attention span today is . . . I have to say this rather quickly or I'll lose you . . . The average attention span today is 9 seconds. Nine seconds! That is, if you're not saying something every 9 seconds that involves and holds your listener, the mind will have a tendency to wander.

Some attribute this short attention span to the advent of the TV remote. Studies have found that some remote users change stations as often as twenty-two times a minute, or once every 2.73 seconds. Of course those who have grown up playing video games have notoriously short attention spans. But these are not the only reasons for our difficulty holding the attention of listeners in an oral environment. The difficulty is intrinsic to the situation.

The mind is capable of processing information at approximately 800 words per minute. The average speaker speaks at 130 to 150 words a minute. Some speakers "gust up" to 180 words per minute or more—but that's still a far cry from 800 words.

Can you see a problem? The mind is able to process information at 800 words a minute. The pastor's preaching at 130 words or so per minute. What happens in between? The mind wanders. It's not that people don't want to listen to us. It's not that they don't like us. It's simply what happens in an oral situation. Unless you are doing something to continually involve your listener, the mind has a tendency to wander. And the situation is not getting better in this digital age when people are accustomed to so much visual stimuli. What shall we do? I'm glad you asked.

Effective oral communication today is aimed at both sides of the brain. You undoubtedly have some knowledge concerning right brain/left brain research. I would like to refresh your memory just a bit. This can have such an enormous impact on the effectiveness of preaching.

The brain is divided into halves. These halves are almost mirror images. Most of our bodily functions are duplicated on both sides of the brain. We have a spare brain almost. That is why stroke victims who have lost, say, the use of an arm, if they go through proper therapy, may regain almost total use of that arm. It's because the other side of the brain takes over some of the functions of the injured arm. It's a beautiful and wonderful way in which God has created us.

In the 1960s, there was an important effort to help people who had life-threatening epileptic seizures. These were seizures that were no long controllable by Phenobarbital, Valium, or any other drugs. One of the experiments on those suffering these seizures involved cutting away parts of the brain. There was a young woman pastor in one of my seminars years ago who had parts of her brain cut away during the '60s in an attempt to stop her seizures.

Roger Sperry and his associates were part of this valiant effort to solve seizures through surgery. One method they experimented with was the severing of the *corpus callosum*, the thick band of nerve fibers that divides the cerebrum into left and right hemispheres. It is this band of nerve fibers which connects the left and right sides of the brain, allowing for communication between the two hemispheres. This procedure of severing those fibers did seem to help some people with epilepsy.

However, Sperry and his associates were concerned what effect this surgery would have upon people's behavior and their ability to learn. After all, they were tampering with the brain. The discovery was that it had very little effect. However, researchers discovered as they studied the two sides of the brain, that the two sides seemed to process information slightly differently. The left brain tended to be more logical, analytical, linear, sequential, verbal and explicit, whereas the right side of the brain tended to be more intuitive, creative, visual, playful and holistic. Now we can make too much of this. These differences are not as pronounced as they are sometimes portrayed.

Nevertheless, Sperry and his associates discovered that most people tend to be dominant in either left-brain thinking or right-brain thinking. Some of this may be congenital; some of it could be cultural. Some of it could grow out of our experiences or our training.

Explaining how people respond to messages by dividing them into left-brain and right-brain groups is a generalization, of course, and an over-simplification. But it has become a convenient way of describing how people deal with information.

I am, for the most part, a left brain person. The material you're reading follows a fairly rigid, linear development, as you have already probably noticed. That's the way I think. I have to work at using the right side of my brain. My experience is that most pastors are left-brain dominant. We are that way by nature, and we are that way by training.

Classical preaching has been aimed at the left side of the brain. This is the way most of us were trained to preach. It goes all the way back to Aristotle and his remarkable work on rhetoric. The Aristotelian model for communication has been the dominant model for oral communication in Western culture for hundreds of years. Preaching, as most of us have experienced it, has been based on this model. The emphasis in classical preaching has been on logic, unity, and coherence—or, depending on your tradition—exegesis, exposition, and application. This is the legacy of our seminary training.

Now, I don't want to sound pejorative, but probably the worst possible place to learn to preach is the theological seminary. Not because homiletics professors lack dedication; they certainly do not. I treasure my homiletics training. But seminary can be hazardous to preaching.

I attended seminary in Washington, D.C. Candidates for the ministry were all men back then; today, the student body is at least 50% female. Many of the men came from the mountains of West Virginia.

I was standing in the lobby of one of the dorms one day, and I overheard a conversation that I will never forget. One of the young men from West Virginia, a graduating senior, was talking about his ministry in the mountains of his home state.

"I was a boy wonder," he said chuckling. "People would come from miles around. I was only 17 years of age, but we had hundreds of people for every revival service I ever preached. And at the close of every service, the altar was filled. I bet I had over a thousand converts my first couple of years of preaching. I didn't have any idea what I was doing. I was really rough. Terrible sermons. I sure know better now." And he gave a hearty laugh.

I wanted to ask him, but I was too timid, "Are people being converted in your services now?"

For many of us, seminary was a time of purging unsophisticated thinking and methodology, and that's good. In fact, that's essential. But where are we now? Is there fire on the altar when we stand up to preach? Are lives being changed and entire communities being redeemed?

But that's not the main problem with learning to preach in a seminary environment. The real problem falls under Marshall McLuhan's time-honored bromide, "the medium is the message."

Thomas Boomershine, who has so many important things to say about story-telling, has a theory to which I subscribe whole-heartedly. Here's his theory: *whatever the dominant medium of communication is in a culture will determine how the gospel is preached and how it is heard.* [9] Think about that for a moment.

What is the dominant medium of communication in a seminary community? I can't say what it is today, but when I was in school, it was the lecture or the printed page. What did you spend most of your time doing in seminary? You spent your time either reading books or listening to lectures. Even worse, what is a lecture except the printed page expressed orally? A seminary professor does not speak off the top of his/her head. He or she has worked out the course material in a very orderly, sequential, analytical, left-brain way before presenting it. I'm generalizing, of course, and it isn't true of every professor. But, we do spend most of our time in a seminary community being primarily logical and analytical. We learn to write well-thought out papers. In short, we learn to speak to the left side of the brain.

All well and good when you are in a seminary community. The problem occurs when we step outside the seminary community. The dominant medium of communication in our general culture today, outside the seminary walls, is no longer the printed page, is it? The dominant medium of communication in our general culture is television. (Digital content on a computer screen, smart phone, PDA, etc. follows the same basic principles as television, except it is more interactive. The implications of this trend have yet to be fully explored, but we will come back to it.)

Now, follow me closely for the next few moments. Television is strictly a right-brain medium, from the word Go. When the television signal enters your home, it is translated by your receiver into a series of dots. If your brain operated differently, that is all you would see on your television screen, a series of dots. But your mind and your eye fashion those individual dots into a meaningful picture, and then your eye and your brain translate those individual pictures into a meaningful story. Most of that is happening on the holistic, playful, visual, creative side of your brain. You're organizing dots into pictures, and you're organizing pictures into a story.

An even better example is animation. Think for a moment about how cartoons are made (at least, before computer animation). The process begins with a series of drawings, perhaps thousands of them, and then these individual drawings are transferred to individual frames of a film. Then these individual frames of the film pass in front of a light and are projected onto a screen. However, we don't see the individual drawings when we look at the screen, do we? We see a cartoon character come to life and we involve ourselves in a story. How does that happen?

Go back with me to Psychology 101 and Festinger's Theory of Cognitive Dissonance. The brain fills in gaps. When you watch that animated film, the holistic, playful, visual part of your brain takes the material you give it—suspends its critical, analytical, and logical other half—and you become involved in the story.

Television and, indeed, all mass media are right brained media, and becoming more so all the time. According to an analysis by Lawrence Baines, mass media is rapidly moving us from a word-based culture to an image-based one. The move toward grander spectacle through computer-generated images moves film even more toward the visual and farther away from the linguistic. The complete dialogue for the first *Terminator* film, notes Baines, which served as a harbinger for a new era of special effects, was just 3,850 words—about as long as a typical magazine article. [10]

Television is a right-brain medium. So, here is our difficulty. We have been trained to preach left-brain sermons to a world that is becoming increasingly right-brain. We are preaching logical, well-supported sermons to a post-modern world that has rejected logic, science and philosophy as absolutes and relegated them to the status of mere sign posts.

Of course, an element of this has always been true. When you and I present left-brain material—logical, linear, analytical, sequential—such material might be convincing, but it does not capture the imagination. It does not touch the heart. Only when we insert a parable, a metaphor, a vivid image, or some kind of story with drama, suspense, and gripping imagery do we really involve the listener in the message. It's not simply a matter of being more entertaining. It's a matter of causing the whole brain to focus on the material being presented.

The effective communicator today will seek not so much to persuade as to involve. He or she will make a conscious effort to appeal to the right side of the brain with plenty of visual imagery. He or she will move not so much from point to point, as from picture to picture. That is why PowerPoint® slides have become a significant tool in preaching as well as video clips. But these are not as important as the visual imagery that fills the content of the spoken word.

The emphasis will not be on abstract logic but on concrete illustration. We will take our preaching style not from the pagan Aristotle but from Jesus the Jew. Jesus was a Jew, you know, and the Jewish faith has traditionally been very concrete in its communication.

I will never forget having a Conservative rabbi in one of my seminars years ago. I asked him to have a blessing before we broke for lunch. Before he acceded to this request, however, he made his way down to the hotel restaurant to borrow a piece of bread to bring up to the room so that he could place it in front of him in order to perform the blessing. Why? Because he did not do abstract blessings. He blessed a particular piece of bread. That is the Jewish way of doing things.

Jesus was a Jew and his communication was concrete, not abstract. He didn't talk about abstract principles. He gave concrete examples. Jesus was very visual, very right-brained, very holistic in his communication. How did we get away from that? He used concrete examples, not abstract theology. Look through the Bible sometime. There is very little abstract theology until you get over to Paul's writings. Who influenced Paul? The Greeks.

I had a great privilege in the 1980s of addressing a national meeting of Conservative rabbis and lay people. It was my understanding that, at that time, most Conservative and Reformed Jewish seminaries did not have homiletics teachers. They imported Christians, generally from leading Protestant seminaries to teach homiletics—which produced an interesting phenomenon. The sermons of Conservative and Reformed rabbis sounded very much like the sermons of mainline Protestant preachers of the time—abstract, logical, linear, etc.

I told some of the rabbis that I had a dream one night. The Pope and the President of the National Council of Churches and the President of the Southern Baptist Convention and a few other Christian leaders got together. They asked the age-old question, "What are we going to do about the Jews."

One of them said, "Well, I'll tell you what we could do to slow them down enormously."

The others asked, "What's that?"

He said, "We'll teach them to preach like Christians, and that way nobody will listen anymore."

The group decided, "That's a brilliant plan." So that's what they have been doing over the past century.

But then those same leaders in my dream got together again and one of them said, "Well, we slowed down the Jews, but you know Christians aren't doing very well either. What are we going to do about Christian preaching?"

And somebody said, "I know, we'll teach them to preach like Jews. We'll teach them to tell stories and to use concrete language and imagery. We'll teach them to infuse their sermons with humor and striking rhetorical devices such as hyperbole and paired elements." And that is what is happening in our better seminaries today. It is also the goal we will seek after in this book. We will try to help you preach like Jesus.

"Jesus never said anything to them without using a parable" (Mark 4:34). You simply cannot improve on that method.

Tell Me a Story!

When *Time* magazine first came on the market, many intellectuals told Henry Luce, the publisher, that it was not a very intellectual magazine—there were too many stories about people. Henry Luce said, "I'm not the first one to tell people stories. I got the idea from the Bible."

There are 64 parables in the New Testament. That is 52% of the content of the synoptic Gospels. Actually, from the beginning of the Bible, what do we have? Story after story after story: Adam and Eve, Cain and Abel, Noah, the Tower of Babel, Abraham and Isaac and Jacob and Joseph and Samuel and David and Solomon and Isaiah. Story after story after story. And why is that true?

For one thing, our faith was transmitted orally for many generations before anybody ever wrote it down. A wandering tribe of Hebrews traveling through the desert one day come upon an ancient Babylonian ziggurat that has fallen in ruins on the desert sand. Around the campfire that night, a Hebrew father turns to his son and tells him the story his father before had told him. How once upon a time, there was a group of people who would build a tower to the heavens that they might make a name for themselves.

That's the way those stories were transmitted for perhaps hundreds or thousands of years before anyone ever wrote them down.

Look at the New Testament. Depending upon which scholar you subscribe to, it was at least a generation after the death and resurrection of Jesus before any of the gospels were transcribed. Before then, the life, ministry, death and resurrection of Jesus were preserved in the memories of his followers and in their preaching.

How could they remember his teachings 30, 40, or even 50 years after his death?

Jesus, as far as we know, never wrote a word, except on that occasion when he wrote in the dirt in the presence of the woman caught in the act of adultery. So, how do we have a record of his teachings?

Easy. Jesus "did not say anything to them without using a parable." In other words, he never talked without a story. So, his followers could easily remember his teachings a full generation after the fact.

We can remember stories, can't we? We may not be able to remember all the laws and the codes of Scripture. Have you ever tried to memorize the Book of Deuteronomy or Leviticus? It would be difficult. In fact, you will recall that the children of Israel lost the books of the law for many generations until they were recovered in the time of Ezra and Nehemiah. Then we have that beautiful picture in Nehemiah 8. Ezra the priest stands and reads the law all day long and the people also stand and weep for joy as the law is being read. Why? Because while the law was lost, it was lost. The stories, on the other hand, could be told from generation to generation without anything being written down.

But it goes more deeply than simply the memorability of the stories. *The Scriptures elevate the oral medium.* David Buttrick's fine book, *Homiletic*, makes a strong case for the oral nature of our faith. Buttrick reminds us that, as far back as the second commandment in the Decalogue, the Israelites were prohibited from making images. Words, not pictures or idols, would be the form by which the faith would be preserved. [11]

How does the *Shema* begin? "Hear, oh Israel, the Lord your God is one God." Not "look" or "touch," but "hear." The faith was to be an oral faith.

That's not an entirely new idea to you. You've probably preached at some time or another on the powerful and creative Word of God. In the beginning, God spoke and said, "Let there be light," (Genesis 1:3) and behold, there was light. And later in the Prophets,

"The Lord has sent a word against Jacob, and it will fall on Israel . . ." (Isaiah 9:8).

The word moved with power in the time of the prophets, "The lion has roared. Who will not fear? The Lord God has spoken. Who can but prophesy?" (Amos 3:8)

And in the Prologue to John's Gospel, "In the beginning was the Word and the Word was with God and the Word was God and the Word became flesh and dwelt among us" (1:1 and 1:14).

And then over in Romans 10:17, we read, "Faith comes by. . ." what? By hearing! Not tasting or touching or smelling. "Faith comes," says Saint Paul, "by hearing." A few verses before that, Paul makes his very plaintive plea, "How can they hear without a preacher?" (10:14).

The writer of Hebrews crowns our discussion: "For the word of God is alive and active. Sharper than any double-edged sword, it penetrates even to dividing soul and spirit, joints and marrow; it judges the thoughts and attitudes of the heart" (4:12).

Calvin Miller reminds us that the late Malcolm Muggeridge in his essay *Fourth Temptation of Christ* alleged that Jesus' fourth temptation was thirty minutes of prime-time television. Muggeridge said that Jesus rejected the offer because faith had always been an otic (a hearing) rather than an optic (a visual) experience. [12] Why is preaching important? Because that's how most people come to faith, by hearing. So, what is the task of preaching? To bring people to faith through the spoken word. We do that best through story.

But there is a third reason story is at the heart of our faith and our preaching. Story is central to our theology. That is, Christian faith is not a philosophy. Nobody sat down and thought up the Christian faith as an explanation for why things are the way they are.

Biblically, our faith is not even a coherent theology. When somebody dies in your church and you go to comfort the family, do you tell them that their beloved went to be with Christ immediately or do you tell them that their loved one lies in the grave until the last day when the trumpet shall sound and all the dead in Christ shall rise? Which view of the Resurrection do you give them? Biblically, you can make a case for either or both, could you not?

Now, that disturbs some people, but to me, that makes the Scriptures more credible. Nobody sat down and tried to iron out all the wrinkles in Scripture. This is an encounter of humanity and divinity and each person wrote from his or her own experience. So, when it comes to describing God, all of us are blind persons trying to describe an elephant. Why? Because God is beyond space and time. How do you visualize a Being that is beyond space and time? I'm still with the little kid who's asking, "Mommy, who made God?"

What was before God? I can't even visualize eternity, can you? Space and time are categories beyond my brain's capacity to encapsulate. So, you have God, who is beyond space and time and you have humanity, creatures of space and time. How does God communicate with us? "The Word becomes flesh and dwells among us."

Why? Because that's all we can deal with: our five senses. Everything else is speculation. The Bible is not a book of philosophy but of revelation. "Taste and see that he is good . . ." (Psalm 34:8).

[I said that in a seminar one time and a young pastor came up to me and said, "That's Von Rad." I said, "I don't care if it's Von Rad, Van Cliburn or United "Von" Lines, to me it is self-evident.]

But once the word becomes flesh, what do we have? We have story. That's the way God chose to communicate with us because that's the only way we could ever receive God's message and be moved by it. Story is right at the heart of everything we believe about God. Stories are a powerful way to communicate. Think about some of the things stories do for us.

Stories connect us to our past. I had an uncle who died some time ago. I hadn't seen my uncle in many years. I hadn't seen some of my cousins on that side of the family in 20 or 30 years. We stood at the graveside after the funeral. What do you think we spent most of our time doing? Swapping stories, things my uncle had been doing, things my cousins had been doing. That was our way of connecting with our past.

Stories also tell us who we are. Psychology tells us that our basic personality is formed before we start school. At five years of age, our personality is not formed by the things we've read, but from primal experiences we had as little children. Those primal experiences come to us in the form of stories. That is, as little ones we looked around and saw how people around us were behaving and that taught us what was appropriate or inappropriate behavior. Sometimes those impressions were in error.

Has it ever bothered you that people who are abused as children sometimes grow up to abuse others? That doesn't make sense, does it? You would think that a person who has been abused as a child would be the last person who would abuse someone else. Could it be, though, that our earliest experiences have such a devastating impact on our perception of reality that we never quite recover?

I have a real fear of heights. I wonder if it had anything to do with the fact that when I was a toddler, I tumbled off a porch at my home and hit my head on a concrete sidewalk, requiring several stitches. Could it be that this initial experience of falling had such a traumatic impact on me that every time I get near a precipice, I relive that experience? The stories we've witnessed and the stories we've participated in as children are powerful forces in our lives today.

Also the stories we have heard. All of us grew up hearing stories didn't we? For example, I often wonder how many girls grow up in our culture with a highly-idealized view of romantic love, because of the fairytales they've heard about Prince Charming sweeping the beautiful princess off her feet. I wonder how many girls grow up waiting for Prince Charming to come along to solve their problems. They wait . . . and they wait . . . and they wait. Finally, they go ahead and marry because reality does not measure up to fantasy. Stories are powerful.

When I was growing up, I heard stories about my grandfather on my mother's side who was a supply pastor in the Methodist church. He was circuit riding preacher. My mother and father met when my grandfather was appointed to a small Methodist church where my father had been playing the organ since he was 14. Do you think that hearing those stories about my grandfather, the supply preacher, had some impact on my choice of vocation?

We are impacted by the stories we witness and the stories we participate in as well as the stories we've heard. These stories tell us who we are. They define appropriate behavior. They may either damage us for life or they may empower us by giving us healthy models to emulate.

We had a true story in *Dynamic Preaching* years ago about a man who had been a Civil War hero. He regaled his sons with his stories of his exploits in the war. His stories had such an impact on his sons that they all joined the military. Not only did they become military men, but their sons did as well, and then their sons, the hero's great grandsons. And then one day somebody did a little bit of research and discovered that great granddaddy never served in the Civil War at all. He had paid somebody to take his place. But he was so embarrassed about this that he moved to a new community and developed a limp and told everyone who would listen the stories of his exploits. The stories weren't true, but the impact on his sons and his grandsons and even his great grandsons was enormous.

Most of us have these family stories. They tell us who we are. To a certain extent they may even define our personality. That's the power of story. These images stored in our brain can have an amazing impact on us.

Stories also connect us to one another. We have certain stories that we tell as a culture. We tell of Washington at Valley Forge and Lincoln at Gettysburg and those unnamed soldiers hoisting the flag on Iwo Jima. This is why you can't talk to some people intelligently about a subject like patriotism. They're not thinking in terms of logic; they're thinking in terms of pictures—Washington, Lincoln, Iwo Jima, Desert Storm, Vietnam, Afghanistan. Nobody dies for a country on the basis of pure logic. They do it because of these images stored in the brain. Stories connect us as denominations, as communities, as ethnic groups. One thing Alex Haley did for the African-American community was to give it *Roots*—stories they could tell about their heritage.

God created *Homo sapiens* to be story-telling creatures. Gregory Bateson tells about a man who wanted to know about artificial intelligence (AI). He went to his own state-of-the-art computer and asked it, "Do you compute that you will ever think like a human being?" The machine then set to work to analyze its own computational habits.

Finally, the machine printed its answer on a piece of paper, as such machines do. The man ran to get the answer and found, neatly typed, the words: "That reminds me of a story." The computer was right. This is indeed how people think. [13]

In fact, there is a book titled *Tell Me a Story: Narrative and Intelligence* by Roger Schank. It is not about stories at all. It is about artificial intelligence. The premise is that artificial intelligence is only possible once a computer can tell and understand stories. Schank makes the point several times that learning only occurs when we reexamine and rewrite our own stories or add new stories. It seems that storytelling and story understanding are at the core of intelligence. [14]

Chuck Swindoll says this about stories: "Stories transport us into another world. They hold our attention. They become remarkable vehicles for the communication of truth and meaningful lessons that cannot be easily forgotten. If a picture is better than a thousand words, a story is better than a million!" [15]

In the 1960s, there was a popular Broadway musical, *Camelot*. It was about King Arthur and his Knights of the Round Table. Arthur tried to build the ideal kingdom. Before this time, knights had roamed freely through the countryside—sometimes pillaging, looting, and causing all kinds of mayhem. But Arthur brought them together and tried to use them for a force for justice, purity and truth. It was a Utopian vision. They had a round table because all the knights were to be equal, none was to be superior to the others. They were to share and they were to behave in such a way as would be beneficial to the kingdom.

But you remember that the serpent was active in Camelot just as in the Garden of Eden, and just as it is in our lives. Guinevere, Arthur's beloved queen, fell in love with Lancelot, his most trusted knight. Negative forces within the kingdom used that tragic situation to splinter the kingdom. And Camelot fell. It became divided into warring rivalries.

There's a very touching scene at the end of Camelot. King Arthur's still very close to Lancelot, and he still loves Guinevere. Arthur's heart is breaking to see this beautiful vision they tried to create torn asunder. He turns to Lancelot and he asks something like this, "Has it all been in vain?" At that point, a young boy comes up beside Arthur and Lancelot and starts tugging on Arthur's robe. This little guy knows all the stories about the Knights of the Round Table and he starts asking Arthur about these stories. Arthurs turns to Lancelot and says that as long as there are little guys like this, who know the stories and can tell the stories, then Camelot will not have been in vain. They'll always remember that "once there was a spot on earth called Camelot." King Arthur closes the story by singing: "Ask every person if they've heard the story, And tell it strong and clear if they have not, That once there was a fleeting wisp of glory called Camelot..." [16]

When I saw that musical and heard those words, I thought, that's our job. That's what we're engaged in. As long as we're telling the story—that once upon a time, the Word became flesh and dwelt among us, then the cross is not in vain. Christ is alive and the kingdoms of this world are becoming the kingdoms of our God. Tell the story. Translate the abstract word of God into the concrete experiences of human beings, and then your work will indeed be blessed.

The Story is the Sermon

Perhaps you've had the experience of sitting in a Bible study and your lay people are talking and one of them says something like, "Oh, it's like that fellow the pastor was talking about Sunday morning. You know, that guy who walked with a limp . . ."

They may have forgotten everything else you said. In fact, they probably did forget everything else you said. Hey, admit it, you may not even be able to remember by Wednesday what you said on Sunday. If they remember anything, it will likely be a story you told. Actor and speaker Max Dixon puts it this way, "Information plus emotion equals memory."

According to communication studies, only 7% of any oral presentation is remembered even hours later. Stories are your best vehicle for exceeding that discouraging statistic.

Procter & Gamble spends more money on advertising than anybody else in the world. Hundreds of millions of dollar each year. Procter & Gamble has a test for their commercials. It's called the 24 Hour Recall—can viewers remember a commercial 24 hours later? Have you noticed that even 30-second spots today tell stories? They don't even try to sell you on the fine qualities of their product. They try to involve you in a story with just a little mention of the product to hook your interest.

Don Hewitt, creator of *60 Minutes*, was once asked about his special talent as a journalist. He said, "My philosophy is simple. It's what little kids say to their parents: 'Tell me a story.' Even the people who wrote the Bible knew that when you deal with issues, you tell stories. The issue was evil; the story was Noah. I've had producers say, 'We've got to do something on acid rain.' I say, 'Hold it. Acid rain is not a story. Acid rain is a topic. We don't do topics. Find me someone who has to deal with the problem of acid rain. Now you have a story.'" [17]

That's not only true of advertising and of commercials. It's also true of sermons. Think back in your own experience. My guess is that most of the sermons you'll remember will be sermons that featured a strong illustration.

When I was a teenager, I was out of church for a while. And then Church Street Church in Knoxville needed a tenor for their choir and they gave scholarships to the University of Tennessee for students to sing in their choir. I needed money badly to go to school. So, that's how I got back in the church—a hired gun singing tenor in the church choir.

It was a terrible burden to put on a college student. Church Street required its singers to sit through both the 8:30 a.m. and the 10:45 service. I had to hear the same sermon twice every Sunday. But the pastor back then was a man named Paul Worley. Paul would tell these beautiful stories, particularly from the Hebrew Bible. He'd talk about Adam and Eve walking in the garden in the cool of the day. You'd picture Eve walking by that apple tree.

I know it doesn't say it was an apple tree, of course, but it's easier to visualize that way. And this tree is just weighed down with those big, red, ripe apples. The serpent whispers in Eve's ear, "Psssst, Eve. Aren't these the reddest, ripest, juiciest-looking apples you've ever seen in your life? God didn't say you couldn't take one of these apples and just hold it in your hand for a minute! Why don't you take one and just hold it, Eve?"

So, Eve takes just one apple. "Doesn't that look delicious? Take a sniff of the aroma, Eve. One little bite isn't going to hurt you. God's not going to punish you for just one little bite."

Paul would tell those stories and for a moment, I was there in the Garden of Eden. To this day I could probably preach some of Paul Worley's sermons verbatim. [Truthfully, as a young pastor I did preach some of Paul Worley's sermons verbatim.] They made such an impression on me and it's been 50 years ago. Paul knew how to tell a story.

I can remember hearing a black pastor from Dallas many years ago, Zan Holmes. Zan was preaching for a Pentecost celebration. He started off his sermon with a very familiar story. He said he flew into an airport one time to speak. He went to the baggage claim area to get his bags. He had been told that someone would come and pick him up in the baggage area and take him to the site where he was to preach.

He waited and waited, but nobody came. Finally, he noticed a man peeking at him around a pillar. The man looked him over real good and finally got up the nerve to come over and speak to him.

He asked, "Are you Dr. Holmes?"

Zan Holmes said, "Yes, I am."

The man said, "Well, you sure don't look like your picture!"

Then Zan Holmes said something like this, "Pentecost is intended to be a picture of what the church should look like." Then Zan Holmes added, "But most of us sure don't look like our picture."

Now, that's the most simple, the most familiar type of illustration. But, that's been over 40 years ago and every time I think of Pentecost, I think of Zan Holmes' experience in the airport that day.

Or I think of a sermon by Dennis Kinlaw of Asbury Theological Seminary that I heard at least 40 years ago on the subject of Malchus' ear. You will find a variation of that sermon on YouTube.

I can't think of a more obscure text in all the scriptures than the story of Malchus' ear. You'll remember Malchus was a servant of the high priest, Caiaphas. In the garden that terrible night when they came to take Jesus, Simon Peter cut off Malchus' ear. Subsequently, Jesus healed that ear. In his sermon, Kinlaw made the point that from that day forward, every time Caiaphas the high priest looked at his servant Malchus and saw that ear that Jesus had healed, Caiaphas would be reminded that once upon a time there was a man named Jesus that he had helped put to death.

Then Kinlaw went on to say that God has placed a Malchus' ear in everyone's life, something to speak to them of the power and the presence of God. It's a sermon on prevenient grace. When I heard that sermon years ago, I didn't even know what prevenient grace was. But, friend, for the rest of my life, prevenient grace will be attached to Malchus' ear. That's a poor choice of words, but you get the idea. I understand a little more about what prevenient grace is because of that wonderful story.

I remember these sermons strictly and solely because of the power of the stories. In that sense, *the sermon is the story.* This is not a book on narrative preaching. Other people like Fred Craddock, Eugene Lowry and many others have already done that—and they have done it far better than I ever could. I am not a writer or a theologian. But I am a story-teller, and I know the power of stories. Sometimes I will tell a story and let that be the outline for my message. Sometimes I use stories to bring light to particular biblical truths. Even though I will never be a pure narrative preacher, I never lose sight of the fact that, ultimately the story is the sermon. Whatever I want people to take away will be wrapped up somehow in a story.

The Hero's Adventure

Stories give us hope. That's one of the reasons we'll always tell stories. Stories inspire us. Perhaps you saw the Joseph Campbell series on PBS few years ago, with Bill Moyers, about the power of myth. A myth is a story that has symbolic and emotional value. A myth may be historically true or it may not. For example, Washington and his troops at Valley Forge is a true story, but it has symbolic, emotional value for us. It's not just dead history. It has taken on the power of myth.

Joseph Campbell said that there is one myth that is more popular than any other across all the cultures of the world. He called it the "Hero's Adventure."

The Hero's Adventure follows a very familiar 3-fold development: a person accepts a great challenge; he [or, of course, she] experiences near defeat or death; finally, he is victorious. Have you ever gone to a motion picture that has followed that pattern?

Can you think of any notable examples of motion pictures that have not followed that progression? *Star Wars, Rocky, Indiana Jones, The Matrix, Transformers, Die Hard*—about every motion picture that Hollywood has ever made has in some fashion or another followed that pattern.

A person accepts a challenge, even if it's simply the challenge of trying to win a girl's heart or to keep a family together during the Depression or whatever it might be. They accept a challenge, experience near-defeat or death, but in the end, they are victorious.

How do you feel when you walk out of a movie that follows that kind of development? You feel great, don't you? You're ready to go out and conquer the world. You're a hero too, vicariously, and you just can't wait to get into action.

Do any of you remember back in the sixties and early seventies when Hollywood tampered with that formula? There were a few movies during that era where, right at the very end, the hero would be killed unexpectedly. Do you remember any of those movies? They didn't make many of them. Why not? How did you feel when you came out of the theater after seeing a movie like that? Depressed. Down. Angry. You wanted to strangle the person who made that movie because it was such a downer. That is the very opposite of the Hero's Adventure. The Hero's Adventure leaves you exhilarated, energized, uplifted.

That is the secret of the Olympics. Who can forget the unexpected and courageous victory of the U.S. Hockey team over the Soviets a few years ago? Of course, they did it again this year, but it wasn't nearly as dramatic. The bigger the challenge, the greater the celebration. There is within us a visceral response when we see anyone set his or her goals high, then encounters obstacle after obstacle, but finally wins the victory.

Little Midori Ito, in the 1992 Winter Olympics figure skating finals, carrying all the hopes of her small island nation on her shoulders, attempts the very difficult triple axel. She spins in the air and makes her landing on the ice. Then she stumbles and everybody goes "Ohhhh," and the tears start trickling down her face because everybody knows she's blown her hopes for the gold medal. But wait, a little later in those same figure skating championships, little Midori Ito gets a second chance. And for the first time in Olympic history, even though she's almost totally fatigued at this point, for the first time in Olympic history, a figure skater tries the difficult triple axel twice in the same Olympics. Little Midori Ito flies across the ice, leaps into the air, turns that little body around, and makes a perfect landing. The crowd goes crazy, and she takes home a silver medal. And we shared in her triumph.

I went to a basketball game the night before one of my workshops. The University of Tennessee was playing Georgia. Georgia had just beaten the mighty Kentucky Wildcats. U.T. was 2 and 8 for the season. But it was on our home floor. We were

The Hero's Adventure

cheering for all we were worth because about 10 minutes to go, U.T. was only 10 points down. But 9 minutes to go, we were 9 points down; 8 minutes to go, we were 8 points down; 7 minutes to go, we were 7 points down. It got down to 2 minutes to go, and we were 2 points down. Twelve seconds to go, U.T. had the ball. Still down by 2 points. They put the ball in Ed Gray's hands, our best shooter. He was wide open for an 18-foot shot. The ball left his hand, and we came to our feet expectantly. The ball touched the rim . . . and then fell away, unfortunately. But after making that comeback, what if he had hit it? What would have happened in Thompson-Boling Arena at that moment if he had sunk a 3-pointer and won the game? People would have gone crazy. You ought to see me when that happens. I'm a raving lunatic at the end of such games. I can live for a week on a high after a game like that.

What's the greatest telling of the Hero's Adventure in history? "Have this mind among yourselves, which is yours in Christ Jesus, who, though he was in the form of God, did not count equality with God a thing to be grasped, but emptied himself, taking the form of a servant, being born in the likeness of men. And being found in human form he humbled himself and became obedient unto death, even death on a cross. Therefore God has highly exalted him and bestowed on him the name which is above every name, that at the name of Jesus every knee should bow, in heaven and on earth and under the earth, and every tongue confess that Jesus Christ is Lord, to the glory of God the Father" (Philippians 2:5-13, RSV).

You recognize that as the *kerygma*, the very heart of the Christian gospel—that Jesus Christ came into this world, suffered at the hands of sinful humanity, died, and on the third day, God raised him from the dead.

For the first 40 or 50 years of the life of the Christian community, that was Christian preaching. They didn't have a New Testament canon. All they had was the *kerygma*—the good news that Jesus Christ came into the world, suffered at the hands of sinful humanity, died, and on the third day, God raised him from the dead.

When Peter preached his great sermon on Pentecost, what did he preach? That same basic message. Can you not imagine that persons who heard those early Christian preachers preach that message of Christ's suffering, death, and resurrection went home feeling uplifted, inspired—feeling that if Christ be raised from the dead, they could live victoriously as well?

Can you imagine that was part of the motivation that sent them into the gladiator pits and caused them to allow themselves to be burned in Nero's gardens without recanting their faith? Can you see that early Christian preaching, which was inspiring hope in people, had the power to motivate them to give their very lives for this new gospel which they proclaimed?

What's wrong with leaving church on Sunday morning feeling lifted up, inspired, victorious—feeling like you can take on the world? Again, I ask, what's wrong with that?

I'll tell you what's wrong with that—that was not the way I was trained. I went to seminary during the late 60s, and friend, if anyone left our churches feeling good about themselves on Sunday morning, we had not done our jobs. We were to "comfort the afflicted and to afflict the comfortable." And my guess is that all we accomplished was to make people angry.

I remember the first sermon I preached in a little white-framed church in a rural area just outside Knoxville. The sermon was titled "Burn, Baby, Burn." I learned some hard lessons in those days, and here is the most important one: If you have people leaving church on Sunday mornings who are angry, depressed, complaining—they are not motivated to do anything except grumble some more. On the other hand, if you have people leaving church feeling lifted up, inspired, hopeful—then they are motivated. They are empowered to move mountains. They believe they can have some impact on the world.

You see, I've fallen under the influence of the outstanding African-American preacher and teacher, Henry Mitchell. Mitchell says that the genius of Black preaching is that it always moves toward a celebration. [18] And what's wrong with that? Why not move your message toward a celebration? Why not accept that pattern of challenge, suffering, and near defeat, followed by God's victory? Why not have that as the pattern for your preaching? It takes work, it takes planning, but why not move your message and your people toward a celebration?

Now, how do you do that? One suggestion is to look for the hero's adventure in the biblical narrative and then simply tell the story.

When You Need to Be Prophetic

They had an expression in the old West: "Smile when you say that, stranger." And if you couldn't smile as you said it, you ran the risk of getting plugged. If people can say something with a smile, it is non-threatening.

Every once in a while, a pastor will write me and say "King, you don't have enough sermons in *Dynamic Preaching* on social justice." And I don't. I plead guilty. But I have many fine excuses. Just kidding. I've learned that we don't really change behavior very well when we confront people and beat them over the head.

Racism is a good example. I'm a Southerner. I've noticed a strange thing. Nobody in the South is a racist. A few years back, David Duke was a household name. Duke was a member of the Ku Klux Klan and a Nazi, but in his eyes, he wasn't a racist. Ted Nugent insists he's not a racist. You can walk up to the most bigoted old fellow in your congregation and ask him, "Are you a racist?" and he'll say, "No, I'm not." There's more denial that takes place on the subject of race than just about any subject in our land. A white guy in Florida can shoot an unarmed black teen—and get off scot-free—and people will say to you with a straight face that race had nothing to do with it.

If you preach a sermon on racism—and I'm not just talking about in the South—lots of denial sets in and nobody hears what you say. That's just the hard truth. So what I try to do is sneak in a story from time to time. One of my favorites was a story that we included sometime back about Stokely Carmichael, the 1960s black radical. The sermon was on anger.

Carmichael was taking his 6-year-old niece to school because they were integrating her school for the first time. A state trooper pulled his gun on Stokely's niece and forced her to the ground. Then he put his boot on her back. This is a 6-year-old child, can you imagine her fear? Stokely Carmichael said something to the effect that the next time a boot was on anybody's back, it would be his boot on somebody else's back.

I could tell that story anywhere in the South and any old bigot sitting out there in the congregation would have to say, "Well, I'd feel the same way." It would appeal to his sense of manhood, if nothing else. For a few minutes, he would be in Stokely Carmichael's skin. And maybe, just maybe, with stories like that, a little change could take place. That may be a cop-out. Maybe I ought to hit oppression and injustice a little harder and more directly, but my experience is that sometimes that is counter-productive.

When I came out of seminary, I was a flaming social prophet, preaching on Amos every Sunday. But my experience is that not much change takes place from such preaching.

We had a large church in our part of the country that had a swimming pool. It was a very wealthy church. They had a day care, and to their credit, they had black children from the neighborhood in that day care. This was in the early 1950s. The day care was going to have swimming lessons in the church swimming pool and that meant integrating the church pool. This was a no-no back then. African-Americans did not use swimming pools that whites used. It was totally unacceptable.

So they had a board meeting, and you can imagine how tense it was. One man, quite influential, was particularly upset. He said, "When it comes down to it, is there anybody in this room that would want to take a bath with a black man?"

The room got deathly still; tension was in the air. Then the most respected man in that church got up—silver haired, distinguished looking, well-to-do. He said, "Gentlemen, there's not a man in this room I'd want to take a bath with. But that's not what's at stake here. There are some little children we need to invite to swim in our pool." And that's all it took. People saw the absurdity of this other person's position, and they integrated that church swimming pool.

Here's the important thing. That story got told in church after church in our part of the country. Every time that story was told, the reaction was the same. And the walls came tumbling down.

Annette Simmons, in her book, *The Story Factor: Secrets of Influence from the Art of Storytelling* tells a familiar Jewish Teaching Story: "Truth, naked and cold, had been turned away from every door in the village. Her nakedness frightened the people. When Parable found her she was huddled in a corner, shivering and hungry. Taking pity on her, Parable gathered her up and took her home. There, she dressed Truth in story, warmed her and sent her out again. Clothed in story, Truth knocked again at the villagers' doors and was readily welcomed into the people's houses. They invited her to eat at their table and warm herself by their fire." [19]

About Narrative Preaching

A person who believes so strongly that the story is the sermon, that meaning must be evoked from within the listener, and that a sermon ought to engage both sides of the brain ought to be a strong proponent of narrative preaching. Yet I resist the purely narrative style.

I remember when I first became enamored with narrative preaching. I had read Tom Troeger's wonderful little book, *Imagining a Sermon*. [20] I began using it in my workshops and selling copies of it at the back of the room—urging pastors to "read this book!" In *Imagining a Sermon*, Troeger introduces us to the narrative style by presenting basically the same wedding homily in two distinct forms—first in the classical style, and then in the narrative. The narrative presentation is a masterpiece. It draws you into the lives of the two people being married in a powerful and unforgettable way. [If you are not able to find Troeger's book, Eugene Lowry has reprinted both versions of this homily in his fine book, *The Homiletical Beat: Why All Sermons Are Narrative*.] [21]

I had already read Fred Craddock's revolutionary texts, *As One without Authority* and *Overhearing the Gospel*. I knew this was the future of preaching, but I was threatened. How could a person as left-brained as I am ever write sermons in this style on a weekly basis? I have still not resolved that tension. But I committed myself to learn as much as I could from these and other highly creative writers on the narrative style.

In narrative preaching, the emphasis is on the emotive as opposed to the purely logical; on the inductive as opposed to the deductive; on a stream of consciousness development as opposed to the old Aristotelian syllogism, and on maximum involvement of the listener.

Narrative preaching is centered in story. Narrative preaching is story. Effective preachers have always used stories to illustrate truth, but in narrative preaching, truth is the story itself. The Word becomes flesh and walks among us—not as an abstract idea, but in a living, breathing representation.

I hope I have fairly represented the basic elements of this art form. I am convinced that we ought to listen to the voices advocating the narrative style and learn from them. Everything they say is important. But my observation is that, unless you are particularly gifted in that direction or you have an extraordinary amount of time for sermon preparation, you will want to adapt some of the narrative techniques without completely employing the narrative style for all your preaching.

I have heard some narrative sermons that left the congregation confused as to the preacher's intent. Yes, I have heard some classical preachers who have left me scratching my head as well. But the deductive style is more easily decipherable mainly because the preacher's purpose is explicitly stated somewhere in the message. Not necessarily so in the narrative style. Maybe I don't give the listener enough credit. And I know that narrative is critical to reaching postmodern minds. But, for many pastors, changing to a totally narrative style will be an elusive goal. Still, there are many lessons we can learn from the narrative preachers. I will list only a few.

Always look for the story. The greatest enemy of narrative preaching in my estimation is the lectionary. So often the texts do not lend themselves to telling a story. You will find, for example, some texts in Paul's writings that are purely propositional and totally lacking in narrative. What are we to do?

Here's what Eugene Lowry suggests. He says, take that passage from Paul and look behind it to the story that produced it. [22] For example, maybe Paul's engaged in a conflict with some of the members of the church at Corinth. Look for the conflict and tell about that conflict by telling the story behind the text. Conflict and tension make the story exciting.

It's much easier with Jesus' teachings. Maybe you're preaching on the story of the dishonest steward. You might begin your message with the question, "Why would Jesus ever choose a dishonest man and make him the hero of the parable?" And then you spend your sermon resolving that conflict. You don't say, "These are some things we want to talk about: a, b, c, d . . ." You involve people in the conflict and you resolve the conflict or the tension that you've created. In resolving the conflict, the sermon will move from scene to scene rather than from point to point. Can you see how much more inviting this would be?

Let's use a very simple example. Let's turn to that familiar story about Jesus and the woman at Jacob's well. When Jesus meets this woman, it's the heat of the day. Now, most people didn't come to the well in the heat of the day, did they? They came in the cool of the morning, or at sunset, because heat in that part of the world can be oppressive. This woman would have to carry her heavy water jug back to her home. Why would she come to the well in the heat of the day?

In the morning, the well was a gathering place for the community. We surmise that she didn't want to encounter other people gathered around the well.

Have you ever known anyone who has gone through life avoiding other people—for whatever reason? Can you think of someone in your frame of reference who has shut themselves off from the world?

I imagine you have some members of your flock who come to church on Sundays, but they'll sit on the back row and then hurry out afterwards so they won't have to talk to anyone. They'll miss the covered dish supper or any occasion where they'll have to interact with others.

Have you ever known older people who've shut themselves up in their house and don't come out for anyone or anything? Have you ever known anyone of any age who's become somewhat of a recluse? Maybe they've had some traumatic experience early in life and they've become withdrawn. They've lived that way so long that now they can't even carry on a decent conversation with anybody else. Maybe they have sunk into a deep depression. Have you ever known anybody like that? As you tell about this woman who came to the well in the heat of the day, could you tell this other person's story as well?

This woman comes to the well at the heat of the day. She's surprised to encounter Jesus. They have a rather extensive conversation, the longest conversation that Jesus has with anybody. It's interesting to note the respect Jesus shows this woman. He not only talks to her, but he also listens to her. They get into a rather deep theological discussion about where God dwells, on a mountain or in the Temple in Jerusalem.

What's surprising about Jesus treating her with so much respect, besides that fact that she is a woman and a Samaritan? It might be the woman's life situation—she's been married five times and is now living with a man who is not her husband. Do you know anyone who has similarly fallen into a less-than-idyllic style of life?

This woman has an encounter with Jesus and it changes her life. Have you ever known anybody like that—someone whose life has been changed by Jesus? Could you tell their story?

How does the story of the woman at the well end? After she has this experience with Christ, she runs to the village to tell other people about this man who has told her everything she has ever done. Isn't that a great way to end the story? At the beginning of the story, we have a woman who's hiding from other people; at the end of the story, she is running to try to find other people so that she can tell them about this man who told her "everything she ever did." This man who swapped her well water for living water.

Isn't that a wonderful way to end a story? Wouldn't it be a wonderful way to end a sermon? You've let the woman's story be the structure of your sermon. You've used an intuitive, emotive stream-of-consciousness development rather than a rigid, ABCD, classical style. And you have ended on a note of celebration.

Tell the biblical story and let the story produce your outline. But look for the hero's adventure and let your message move toward a celebration. Is this the only way to develop a narrative sermon? Not by a long shot.

About Narrative Preaching

There are books by outstanding narrative preachers like Fred Craddock, Eugene Lowry, Thomas Troeger, Calvin Miller, and many others who could take you far beyond this simple beginning, but it is a beginning and it does work.

Usually, those of us with a left-brained orientation will apply narrative principles to an otherwise somewhat propositional presentation. Let me give you an example, if I might.

I once heard a preacher begin a sermon on stewardship with a very simple story. Sadly, I cannot recall the preacher's name. Otherwise I would tell you, for it was a masterpiece.

He was addressing a denominational conference. He painted a picture of a young altar boy lighting the candles for the first time in a worship service. But this young lad's arms and legs were not long enough for him to reach these two lofty candlewicks. He tried as best he could, but he could not get the stick which he carried at an appropriate angle to light those two candles.

This young boy stood for a moment surveying the situation in total despair, then he looked to his parents for support, and of course, they had no idea what to do. A tear began trickling down his face.

The preacher took us to this point in this young man's story, and then he stopped. He told us his denomination was like that helpless child standing in front of the altar. They were trying to reach their financial goals but those goals were just a little out of reach. And he talked about some of their needs, using facts, figures and other supporting evidence.

He did a splendid job, but then at the end of the message, he took us back to our young hero standing helplessly in near defeat in front of that altar, and he told how he watched a sudden inspiration come to this young altar boy.

The young fellow turned his back on the altar and faced the congregation and then, standing on tiptoe, he reached back over his head until the tip of his lighted stick touched the flame to the candle wick. The process of reaching back over his head gave him that extra angle that allowed the wick to be lighted. And then very carefully, the young man moved over to the other candle stick and successfully repeated the same operation. Then he laid down the stick that he was carrying and turned toward the congregation, and with a broad smile of satisfaction on his face, he raised both his hands with his thumbs up. And then he said loud enough for everyone in the sanctuary to hear him, "Yes!"

Then our preacher said, "And I believe that at the end of our current campaign, our denomination, will let out a hardy 'Yes!' as we reach our goals."

That was the conclusion to his message. Did it work? The entire congregation rose and gave him a standing ovation. We had ourselves a celebration—from a stewardship sermon, of all things.

One more example of the hero's adventure—straight out of the headlines. The headlines in *The New York Times* read like this: "'We've Been Waiting,' They Say after 3 Days Underground." It was a wonderful human interest story as well as a preacher's dream come true.

It was about a dramatic mine rescue in Pennsylvania that occurred several years ago. Nine miners were almost miraculously rescued from certain death. The opportunities for using this story in preaching are numerous.

Advent: "The people who walked in darkness . . ." (Isaiah 9:2, NRSV)

Lazarus: "When Jesus arrived, he found that Lazarus had already been in the tomb four days . . ." (John 11:17, NRSV)

Easter: "Therefore command the tomb to be made secure until the third day; otherwise his disciples may go and steal him away, and tell the people, 'He has been raised from the dead . . .'" (Mat. 27:64, NRSV)

And my favorite:

Grace: "For I am convinced that neither death, nor life, nor angels, nor rulers, nor things present, nor things to come, nor powers, nor height, nor depth, nor anything else in all creation, will be able to separate us from the love of God in Christ Jesus our Lord." (Rom. 8:38-39, NRSV)

About Narrative Preaching

Why do I call it a preacher's dream? The primary task of preaching is to make the abstract concrete. It is to translate the mystery of God into the everyday lives of mere mortals. Most lay people, for example, do not understand the word "grace." The task of the preacher is to paint a picture of grace—like Jesus did with the story of the prodigal—and then say, "Look! That is what grace is like."

And so we say, "It is like 9 miners who could no longer help themselves. They were totally dependent on intervention from above . . ."

Like good storytellers, then, we gather as many facts as we are able. Details make a story come alive. The description below is drawn from news stories by Francis X. Clines in *The New York Times* (July 29, 2002) and by Traci Watson in *USA Today* (July 29, 2002). I have selected a few of the bare-bone facts so that you can flesh them out and make them real if sometime you should choose to re-tell the story:

Sunday, July 28. Rescue workers in Quecreek, Pa. broke through a coal-mine wall to nine trapped miners and found them all alive and well and aching to be rescued after three days of fighting for survival in a pocket of air in their flooded mine.

A wave of exultation swept out from the floodlit rescue scene in a farm field here as the first words resounded up from below with the news that all the missing miners had survived their ordeal 244 feet down in the 50-degree cold of the flood waters.

People were weeping and cheering at village roadsides and television sets at the news that the disastrous flood deep underground had left no fatalities among the harried night crew that disappeared on Wednesday deep in the Quecreek mine.

The desperate rescue operation reached the miners after assorted mechanical setbacks and a long, excruciating period of silence from below since Thursday when the noise of rescue operations rendered fruitless any attempt at hearing tapped signals from the men.

The miners, who gasped for air as floodwaters rose to their chins, tied themselves together so all of their bodies would be found if they drowned.

Miner Blaine Mayhugh, 31, asked his boss for a pen when the water in the shaft kept rising. "I said, 'I want to write my wife and kids to tell them I love them,'" he said.

There is much more to the story, but you get the idea. As you tell that story, the abstract ideas of grace and salvation become concrete.

"I pretty much preach one-point sermons," says Louie Giglio, director of Choice Resources and a popular speaker on college campuses. "My goal is to give them one image to take away with them that will help them live their life the rest of the week. And it's all about story, inviting them into God's story, telling about others who joined God's story. They aren't hungry for information—they hunger to know that there is a God who loves them." [23]

A second lesson I've learned from the narrative preachers is to pay attention to the details. People love details.

Richard Dimbleby was a gifted BBC broadcaster, writer and reporter who did more homework than any of his contemporaries before an interview. Once, he was on the air at the Royal Needlework School in London, where the queen mother was to make an appearance. Dimbleby described the items on display, talked about the school's history, and then it came time for the royal appearance.

But the queen mother didn't appear, so Dimbleby went around again, talking about needlework in China, Japan, Persia and Europe, describing different stitches as though he had spent his entire life with a needle in his hand.

The queen mother appeared, 25 minutes late. She explained that she'd been watching Dimbleby on television and had become so engrossed in what he was saying that she had forgotten the time. [24] To pay attention to the details is to take your time telling stories. That's the only way you can drive a story home.

John Claypool tells about a young man from the mountains of Appalachia in World War II who joins the army. Somehow he is assigned to the parachute corps. He's never been up in an airplane before and he is getting ready for his first jump. The young soldiers are sitting with the parachute instructor. He shows them how to fold a parachute and which string to pull. The boy is watching, concentrating more than he's ever concentrated on anything before in his life, because he knows his life depends upon knowing how to pack and how to use that parachute.

That's the way we would like people to listen to a sermon, with just that kind of intensity. They'll do that if we take our time in developing a story, building drama and suspense as we go along. There's a great tendency to hurry through illustrations. Take your time with the story. Even cut down on the verbiage in between stories because the story is what's going to make the impact.

A third lesson I've learned from narrative preaching is to be conscious of the "Zeigarnik Effect." Are you familiar with the "Zeigarnik Effect?" Didn't you get that in homiletics? I'm kidding. The concept doesn't come from homiletics; it comes from psychology.

If you are familiar with the great narrative preachers, you know they have a frustrating tendency not to provide conclusions at the end of their sermons. I mean, when a preacher's finished I like to hear him or her say, "Now, this morning we've talked about a, b, c." I like that kind of closure. It helps me.

Narrative preachers will often not provide closure and that disturbed me until I discovered the Zeigarnik Effect. To tell you about the Zeigarnik Effect, I need to tell a story.

There once lived a psychologist whose last name was Zeigarnik. She was an associate of the great psychologist Curt Lewin. One night, she and Lewin and four of their colleagues went out to dinner in a fancy restaurant. Six psychologists sitting around the table. Can you imagine the conversation? The psychologists had a very polished waiter. When they placed their order, he took no notes. This was a festive occasion. They ordered a large, lavish meal with several entrees. Still, the waiter didn't write anything down. When the food came, everything was just as they ordered it.

When it came time for them to pay, the six psychologists asked for separate checks. Though he hadn't written anything down, the waiter was able to tell them exactly what they had ordered and the exact total for each of their meals. The psychologists were impressed.

They sat there stroking their chins and saying, "Hmmm, this guy's good. This guy's good."

They paid for their meal and started out of the restaurant. They passed the same waiter. Being good psychologists, they decided to test him one more time. So they asked him, "What did each of us order and how much did it cost?"

The waiter could not remember a single order! It was all gone. Up until the time they paid their bill, he could remember everything, but once they paid for their meal, it was gone. Ms. Zeigarnik decided to study this phenomenon. She studied it first with children and then with adults, and here is what she discovered. If you leave something open-ended, people are more apt to remember. When you provide closure, they have a tendency to forget. Now, transfer this to preaching.

My former pastor, Jerry Anderson, years ago preached a wonderful sermon on the Good Samaritan. He gave several wonderful examples of people helping other people. He came to the end of that sermon and he told about an experience that he'd had when he moved to Cleveland, Tennessee, years before. This was his first pastorate right out of seminary. Jerry and his family drove a U-Haul trailer with all of their belongings up to this little parsonage. They unloaded all their stuff, then he and his daughter took their leftover trash to the city dump.

When they got to the dump they were amazed to discover that there was no fence around this small mountain of refuse. They drove into the center of the dump to leave their trash and discovered much to their chagrin a group of little children—four, five, six years of age—scavenging in the garbage. They couldn't believe it. Jerry said his daughter became hysterical. She started screaming, "Daddy, what are you going to about this? Daddy, what are you going to do about this?"

He said, "I tried to calm her down and tell her I couldn't do everything, but she wouldn't let me off the hook. 'Daddy, what are you going to do about this?'" And Jerry told us things his little church had done in response to that situation. They went to the city council, they got a fence built around the dump, they started ministering to the families, etc.

Selina and I were going out of church afterwards and I turned to her and I said, "I wish Jerry hadn't told us what that church did. They were things any church would have done. But once he told us, he provided closure for us. He gave us permission to close the file on that sermon and say, 'Well we heard a good sermon this morning. Next Sunday we'll hear another good one.' But if he had stopped with his daughter screaming 'Daddy, what are you going to do about this?' and just sat down, we would have been finishing that sermon over lunch."

Now, you're thinking, "King, in my tradition I'm supposed to bring folks to the altar on Sunday morning. How does an open-ended sermon fit with my task?" You'll have to wrestle with that. I don't have an answer. But that's what the research indicates. If you leave something open-ended, people have a tendency to remember. Once you provide closure they have a tendency to forget.

You might be thinking, "King, how does that mesh with moving toward a celebration?" It doesn't. I wouldn't use an open-ended approach very often. It would lose its power. Used selectively, however, it might very well open minds and change lives.

Telling the Biblical Story

Great preaching is always grounded in and nourished by the Word. The primary difference between a speech and a sermon is that a sermon grows out of the preacher's encounter with the Word. Does this mean that a sermon has to have a text? I can't decide that for you. Remember, one of the most delightful little books in all of the Bible, the Book of Esther, doesn't mention God at all. Your sermon may not have a text *per se*, but it still must spring from the Word to qualify as a sermon.

I'm definitely not going to argue for a specific kind of biblical preaching. I am simply suggesting that when preaching has a strong biblical foundation, it carries an authority that it does not otherwise have. For those of us who are enamored with storytelling, the greatest stories in all of literature are in the Bible.

How you use the Bible is something that you'll have to hammer out for yourself. Should you follow a lectionary? I expressed anguish over use of the lectionary in the previous chapter. Many great preachers follow the lectionary religiously. Some of you may not have a choice. You either do or you do not, according to your denominational practice. I must tell you that *Dynamic Preaching* follows the Revised Common Lectionary.

There are advantages to following a lectionary. You're forced to look at passages and scripture that you might otherwise overlook. You must look at the entire Bible rather than sections. Your congregation is protected against your preaching your favorite passages to the exclusion of the rest of the Bible. Special seasons receive maximum emphasis. There is a feeling of movement and coherence throughout the church year. And, most importantly, the whole gospel is preached.

For example, I've always wondered what a very liberal lectionary preacher does with all those texts in Advent that refer so explicitly to the second coming. If you follow the lectionary and seek to faithfully expound the word, then you're going to have to struggle with uncomfortable subjects, like eschatology, Ascension, etc. But I'm not advocating preaching from a lectionary. It has its advantages; it also has its drawbacks.

It's more demanding to preach from a lectionary. Some texts are most challenging. You'll find yourself groaning as you wonder why a particular text was ever chosen. There are some texts that, at first glance, seem to have no redeeming value.

An even greater problem that I have already alluded to is the limitation that following a lectionary places on the preacher in finding stories. My own experience is that following a lectionary is more destructive to expository preaching than it is to life-situation preaching. You can always tag a life situation sermon on to a text. But if your favorite approach to preaching is to preach from the great stories of the Bible, you'll find it more difficult following a lectionary.

That's my experience. Yours may be different. However you choose to proceed, the important point is that the Bible is the number one source book for the preacher. The better the preacher, the more reliant he or she is on the Word.

The Bible is your best source of stories—with one caveat. If you are using a Bible story to illustrate a particular point in your message, be sure the people can relate to the story. You don't want to illustrate one unknown with another unknown. I'm assuming that you begin your sermon preparation with the Bible. All preaching is biblical preaching. However, your goal is to relate the biblical story with life today, so you will generally use modern illustrations to illustrate a biblical text.

Having said that, however, some of the biblical stories could come out of today's headlines. The story of David, for example, would make a fascinating ongoing soap opera. It has adventure, violence, sex, murder, and a royal family with relationships as complicated and intriguing as any modern novel or TV series.

There are some reasons why you should use the Bible as a source book of illustrations. For one thing, the Bible stories contain grace. That is, the Bible is not a book of heroes. The Bible is a book that tells about some very weak people who get by with God's help. Abraham, the father of our faith, did some really stupid things but still, because of his faith, he was triumphant.

You also help fight biblical illiteracy when you use the Bible as a source of illustrations. People need to know these stories. There's something special about the Bible that produces spiritual growth in people when they hear Bible preached.

When you use biblical illustrations, it gives your preaching credibility. My experience is that there is at least one person in every church who prides himself or herself on being more spiritual than the pastor. It's difficult to criticize a pastor as unspiritual if he or she chooses stories from the Bible as illustrations. Just make sure the people can relate to those illustrations.

One word of caution. Just as preaching must begin in the Word, it must not end there. The primary function of preaching is to apply the Word to life today. As Harry Emerson Fosdick once wisely noted, "Nobody except the preacher comes to church desperately anxious to discover what happened to the Jebusites." The focus of the sermon is not the text. The focus of the sermon is the application of God's Word to the needs of actual people.

Grady Davis once suggested that the primary difference between Jesus and the Scribes was that the Scribes were always talking in the past tense, teaching about the Biblical past, whereas, Jesus addressed the present. Davis suggests that perhaps we have too many Scribes today who are still preaching in the past tense, who have developed the habit of looking backwards. [25]

One way you can guard against this is to put the story in the present tense. Don't tell the biblical story as if the characters are in bathrobes like we do with Mary and Joseph at Christmastime. Put them in 3-piece suits and evening dresses. Make them as real as the soap-opera characters are in the afternoons. Frederick Buechner, in a sermon about Pilate, put him in a limousine with tinted glass. [26]

If you're talking about David and Bathsheba, we want to see the anguish on David's face as he deals with the aftermath of his lust. Help us feel the treachery as he orders the death of one of his most loyal soldiers. Make David come alive for us and every ear will be tuned in as you seek to ease the numerous conflicts in David's life.

Great preaching is biblical preaching. One thing this means is that the preacher must spend time daily with the Word, not just when he or she is preparing a message. Thirty minutes spent each day in systematic Bible study over several years would make some preachers biblical scholars beyond their wildest dreams.

Read through the Bible at least once a year, making notes as you go along. It will add a richness to your pulpit efforts that ordinary preachers will not have. Be a biblical preacher.

If there's one thing narrative preaching may do for us, it is to restore the joy of biblical preaching. For most of us, the first story we tell will be the biblical story. If we tell that story like good story tellers—and not to simply get it out of the way so we can get on with the important business of the day which is our sermon—our people will be blessed. A good preacher who has learned lessons from the narrative style will take time with the text, exploring the story behind the text in order to make it come alive for the listener. If we'll do that, we'll discover a new joy in telling the biblical story.

The Art of Sermon Illustration

Most preachers are not narrative preachers *per se*. Neither do most preachers satisfy themselves with "three points and a poem." My observation is, however, that propositional preaching is still dominant. Classical outlines still determine the sermon's development. However, preachers from every theological camp are increasingly aware of the power of illustrations. Story-telling is more popular than ever. It has not always been so.

When I started *Dynamic Preaching*, it was in reaction to the sermons contained in a very fine periodical found in mainline seminary libraries in the 1960s, which no longer exists, *Pulpit Digest*. The sermons printed in *Pulpit Digest* were written by people who were considered to be the leading preachers of the day. Each month, I would search *Pulpit Digest* for good stories that I could "borrow" from one of these great preachers to weave into my preaching. Usually, my search was in vain. So I committed myself to spend my professional life finding quality illustrations that pastors could use.

Pastors sometimes say to me, "King, you use too many illustrations in the sermons you publish in *Dynamic Preaching*." Well, duh! That's the reason the publication exists. It is a resource designed to help pastors supplement their sermon preparation, not replace it (these sermons, by the way, are also found at Sermons.com). Now, of course, good story-telling is taking place in pulpits all over our land. Illustration services are ubiquitous. And for good reason. It's a poor sermon today that contains no stirring illustrations.

Bill Hybels, of Willow Creek fame, has said the three principles of effective communication are, "Illustrate, Illustrate, Illustrate." Haddon Robinson has said, "Few words are as welcome from the pulpit as the words 'Let me illustrate.'" Former Vanderbilt professor of Homiletics John Killinger put it like this: "I have never heard a good sermon illustrator who was not at least a passable preacher, and I have never heard anyone who was not able to use illustrations to whom, even a generous listener, would give passing marks."

There is no better way for effective oral communication to take place than through powerful illustrations. There is no better way to engage people in active listening than through powerful illustrations. There is no better way to arrive at mutual meanings than by the words, "Let me illustrate." or, "Let me give you an example." As someone has noted, "In an image-rich age, postmodern preachers should draw on image-rich narratives and stories to present the gospel and make it clear." Amen! There are several reasons why this is so. I'll list only a few.

Illustrations help us clarify. The 6 most important words in the preacher's vocabulary are "Let me give you an example." And friend, if you cannot give an example to support your high and lofty precepts, chances are you don't really grasp what you're trying to get across either.

The editors of the *Encyclopedia Britannica* used to tell their writers that 9 out of 10 people will take a clear statement to be a true statement. In other words, if you can just state the gospel clearly, it will have power. The gospel is revolutionary in every age and every time. We're not living in a post-Christian age. We are still living in a pre-Christian age because no one has ever really, in any generation, taken the words of scripture seriously. We're still living in a pre-Christian world, and what we have to declare is life changing and earth shaking. All we have to do is state it plainly so that there's no question what we've said and it's going to influence people's lives. In Nehemiah 8:8 we read that, when Ezra read God's Word publicly, he made it "clear," and gave the meaning "so that the people could understand what was being read" (NIV).

Do you believe that a pastor would ever deliberately obscure his or her message? I wouldn't have thought so, but many years ago I heard it happen. I went to hear a well-known pastor of a large United Methodist church. He's a very committed pastor. However, he's also very liberal in his theology. The Sunday I heard him, he was following the lectionary, and that particular Sunday the lesson was on one of the healing miracles of Jesus. Now, let me hasten to add that this pastor's sermon was very polished, eloquent, and scholarly. At the same time it was tremendously dull.

What really got my stomach churning after the service was that when I got outside, I had no idea what that pastor really said. I'm a person of at least average intelligence. But I couldn't have told you anything he said in that message. And as I thought that through, I came to this conclusion—what do you do when you're preaching on one of the healing miracles of Jesus and you're not really certain that Jesus ever healed anybody physically or not? In that circumstance, you use language not to clarify but to obscure.

Richard Saul Wurman in his book, *Information Anxiety* says, "Those who know that they are profound strive for clarity. Those who would like to seem profound to the crowd strive for obscurity. He is a thinker; that means, he knows how to make things simpler than they are." [27]

If you will preach the gospel clearly, your preaching will have power. Spurgeon once said that a lot of preachers must think that Jesus said, "Feed my giraffes," rather than "feed my sheep" because they put the food up so high that the laypeople can't get to it. The mad Roman emperor Caligula wrote his laws in very small letters, and hung them up high on very tall pillars, so his people could not access them. Avoid such madness. Illustrations help us clarify.

Illustrations help us relate theology to life. That's the task of preaching, isn't it? It's to take the abstract truth of God and apply it to the concrete situation of human living.

Jesus could have written a book on grace, but what did he do? He gave us the parable of the prodigal son. Since then, thousands of books have been written on grace but none of them have been an improvement on what Jesus did with a simple story. Jesus could have written a brilliant essay on misplaced values, but what did he do? He gave us the story of a man who was going to build bigger and bigger barns so he could say to his soul, "Now eat, drink and be merry." And God comes to this rich man and says, "Thou fool, tonight is thy soul required of you" (Luke 12:20). That was Jesus' method. He took the abstract and presented it in concrete form where everybody could access it.

And this is the task of every preacher—to take the abstract and make it concrete. If Jesus had kept things on an abstract level, he never would have been crucified, would he? Someone asks Jesus, "What must I do to inherit eternal life?" Jesus says, "'Love the Lord your God with all your heart and with all your soul and with all your mind.' This is the first and greatest commandment. And the second is like it: 'Love your neighbor as yourself.'"

If he had stopped there, everything would have been fine. It's a bit abstract, but it is an answer everyone can be happy with. But someone asks him, "Who is my neighbor?" And Jesus tells a story about a man going down the road who falls among thieves and is left beaten and robbed by the side of the road . . . and a priest passes by . . . and a Levite passes by . . . and then a lowly Samaritan comes by, ministers to the man and takes him to a nearby inn (Luke 10:25-37). If Jesus had kept things abstract, he would have been popular with everybody, but as soon as he made the hero a Samaritan, things probably got a little sticky.

Let's get a little closer to home. I'm a Southerner, as I've already noted. Southern preaching at its best is great preaching. But in the South, we preached for 250 years on love and never got across the idea that love had anything to do with the way we treated our African-American neighbors. That's quite an accomplishment, don't you think—to preach for a quarter of a millennium on the parable of the Good Samaritan and never relate it to our neighbors?

I've read that James Stewart, the famous theologian of the World War II era, wrote voluminously during that time, but somehow did not mention the World War. His sermons were clever and erudite, but young people were being slaughtered on the battlefields of the world and he took no note of it. Amazing. The task of preaching is to take the abstract word of God and make it concrete so that nobody can miss the point. If you keep things on an abstract level, you never have to worry that you're going to offend somebody, but you're not going to save anybody either.

Illustrations make dry facts real. I was leading a workshop in Boston years ago when a moose got loose in a suburb of that great city. This was an enormous animal with a gigantic rack on its head. The police didn't know what to do with this huge animal. They cornered and corralled it, but they still didn't know what to do with it. They couldn't transport it without immobilizing it. They called the zoo. The zoo said it would be a little risky to try to tranquilize an animal of that size, and the zoo refused to have anything to do with it. They were afraid that it would cause some damage or hurt somebody and they might be liable. So finally, the police, not knowing what to do, shot and killed the moose. You can imagine the uproar in Boston because the police shot that moose.

Next Sunday morning, you can stand in the pulpit and say to your people that there are 40,000 children dying every day of illnesses related to malnutrition and you won't get nearly the response from them that a moose getting loose in Boston got.

You can have a whale beach itself somewhere and suddenly you'll have helicopters flying overhead and the National Guard involved. But you talk about 40,000 children dying of malnutrition and nothing happens. The only way anything is going to happen is to take those 40,000 children and bring them down to one little girl that you saw living in a cardboard box in a rundown section of town, scrounging with her baby brother in a garbage can to find food. Give her a name and a face and a swollen belly—then maybe you can get folks concerned. But if you never personalize it by taking those 40,000 children and telling the story of one little girl, you will never get your people to respond. It just won't happen. That's the way we are. I don't know why, but it seems to be a part of human nature.

Peter Tilley, President Bush's representative to the Convention on the Rights of the Child held in 1991 at the United Nation's building in New York City, pointed out that if 40,000 spotted owls were dying every day, there would be a public outrage. However, 40,000 children die each day and no one notices.

Tilley made another analogy that was quite vivid. He said if a hundred Boeing 747 airplanes, each one carrying 400 people crashed each day, the government would take action. However, an equal number of children die of malnutrition, and there is no comment from the government or, we might add, from Christian congregations.[28] Images and stories have an awesome ability to move people to action.

On a cross-country flight some time back, I saw the beautiful and moving motion picture, *Awakenings*. *Awakenings* is the true story of a doctor in Baltimore, Maryland, who found a way to help people who were left catatonic, almost zombie-like, by the 1917–28 epidemic of *encephalitis lethargica*. The doctor found that by giving these patients L-dopa, he could reach them . . . at least temporarily. This was back when L-dopa first started being used to treat Parkinson's disease.

However, the head of the hospital would only let the doctor experiment on one patient because L-dopa was very expensive at that time. The patient that was selected, Leonard, made what seemed to be a miraculous recovery. In light of Leonard's progress, the doctor wanted to administer L-dopa to all the rest of the patients.

The administrator asked how much this was going to cost. The doctor figured it would be about $12,000 a month. The administrator said they couldn't do that, they didn't have the funds.

The doctor asked if he could go to the patrons of the hospital and ask their help. The administrator said the patrons were already giving as much as they could afford. "Well," said the doctor, "maybe I can introduce them to Leonard. Would that make a difference?" The administrator said he didn't think it would change their minds at all.

The doctor and the administrator are sitting at a cafeteria table having this conversation and suddenly and quietly other workers in the hospital start coming up and laying checks on the table. You see, they had met Leonard and they wanted to help. The administrator changes his mind. Maybe, he says, it's worth a try. And so the doctor presents Leonard to the patrons of the hospital and shows the change that has taken place in Leonard. The patrons start writing checks like crazy so the other patients can have L-dopa as well.

Pastor, here is the question you need to ask in every sermon: where is my Leonard? Illustrations take dry facts and make them real.

Illustrations intensify the emotional level of the message. As Guy de Maupassant pointed out, audiences cry to message-givers:

"Comfort me, Amuse me, Touch me, Make me dream, Make me laugh, Make me weep, Make me shudder, Make me think."

I hope you realize I'm not talking about emotionalism or cheap manipulation. To me, that's not only repulsive, it's counterproductive in today's environment. Having said that, however, we are sophisticated men and women. We know that people rarely make their decisions on the basis of dry facts alone. We are not strictly, or even primarily, logical creatures. If we were, the world would run absolutely beautifully. But it doesn't run absolutely beautifully because nobody makes decisions on a purely logical basis.

You probably didn't buy your last car on a strictly logical basis. You might have bought a Chrysler because your father drove a Chrysler. In your mind, you may think that a Honda would be a better investment, but somehow that would seem disloyal. And so you went ahead and bought a Chrysler.

You didn't choose your spouse on a purely logical basis. And I know your spouse didn't choose you. Just kidding, of course. We don't make decisions in a strictly rational way.

Like most people, I love to eat. Thank God, literally, that I got involved years ago with a Senior Olympic basketball team. That is the only way I keep my weight under control. I have very little discipline when it comes to food. You can give me a lecture on the dangers of being overweight and I'll listen and I'll nod and agree with you, but I probably won't change my behavior unless you can paint a picture of me weighing 400 pounds and scare me to death or, conversely, paint a picture of me looking lean and trim like I was in high school, a picture so attractive that I want to conform to it.

Raw information is not enough. We're rarely moved by rational thought. We are moved from the gut, from the feeling level. You can resist that truth all you want. But people are motivated more by the heart than by the head. We dare not overlook the importance of emotion in determining human behavior. Illustrations provide for us the opportunity to intensify the emotional level of our message.

In his seminars, motivational speaker Tony Robbins talks about the power of strong metaphors. He tells about a counselor who was working with a family who had a son enslaved by alcohol and drugs. The parents hesitated to take strong action because, they said, they were afraid it would drive him away and because they respected his freedom.

The counselor said this to those worried parents: "There are two bullets pointed at your son's head right now. One of them is drugs, the other is alcohol, and one or the other is going to kill him—it's only a matter of time—if you don't stop him now." They took action.

Advertisers are very conscious of the power of vivid images to change behavior. "The children of this world are wiser than the children of light" (Luke 16:8). Now, who said that? Advertisers know that in order to change behavior, they have to go through a specific cycle. Information comes into our brain, then the brain translates it into an image, then that image is anchored to an emotion, and both the image and the emotion are tied to changed behavior.

If you're going to change behavior, you have to go through that entire cycle. You've got to hit the mind, then the heart. And then maybe—and just maybe, because people are very difficult to change—some changed behavior will take place. In other words you want to take a holistic approach to the Gospel, using both emotional and logical content.

In the early depression, *Little Orphan Annie* was the most popular comic strip in this nation. Aside from appearing in newspapers across the nation, it was dramatized on radio and in two movies. A blizzard of letters steadily descended on Harold Gray, Annie's creator.

He once had Annie lose her dog, Sandy. Among the anguished letters that came in was a telegram. It read like this, "Please do all you can to help Annie find Sandy, stop, we are all interested, signed Henry Ford." [29]

Illustrations capture the heart as well as the head and thus they are critical to effective communication.

Illustrations help us establish rapport. What a beautiful word, rapport. Rapport between the pastor and the congregation is a very powerful thing. For example, if you were to be out of the pulpit next Sunday and your people knew about it in advance, attendance would probably drop just a little bit even if you have a really fine guest preacher. Unless you have made them mad at you, for most of your people, church on Sunday is you standing in the pulpit. Now, that may or may not be altogether healthy, but the rapport between pastor and people is a very powerful part of the communication process.

Illustrations are one way we build rapport, particularly when we use personal illustrations. Every personal illustration involves some degree of self-revelation, and if that self-revelation comes across in a positive way, people are drawn to you. They begin to trust you because they feel they know you. And that's powerful.

Illustrations give the sermon a wider audience. Now, what do I mean by a wider audience? Let's go back to those 6 most important words, "Let me give you an example."

I was speaking in Chattanooga, TN, several years ago to a family camp being held in a state park. There were several hundred people in attendance. The setting was a large, semicircular, outdoor amphitheater, and on the front row was a beautiful group of third-, fourth-, and fifth-graders. They were sitting there like little birds on a power line with their mouths wide open. It was a delightful experience.

After the second service, a woman came to me and said, "King, you know why those children are sitting there on the front row, don't you?"

I said, "No I don't."

She said "It's your stories, they love the stories."

Well, I found that out the hard way. The last service, I had a message which was designed primarily for the adults and had few stories in it. Believe me, I lost those children. I don't mean I just lost them figuratively. I lost them literally. They started scooting out the end of the row, and by the end of that message, there wasn't a single child left in that amphitheater. They were all out in the woods playing. That taught me a lesson. Children are not the only ones, of course, who respond to stories. Old folks respond to stories, teenagers respond to stories.

In most churches, most of the worship service is aimed at middle-aged adults. The only time we're going to be able to involve our children or youth in the worship experience is with the stories we tell. Think back to when you were a sixth-grader. What kept you listening? And who is more important in that worship experience than those fourth-, fifth- and sixth-graders? Who has more decisions to make and more problems to face than they do? Stories, illustrations, are the way we keep them involved in the message.

Illustrations also make it easier to preach without notes. The esteemed pastor John A. Redhead carefully wrote every sermon he ever preached. He familiarized himself with it thoroughly. Then, he refused to take a single note into the pulpit—on the grounds, he said, "that paper is said to be a poor conductor of heat."

A 55-year-old pastor friend of mine took a manuscript into the pulpit every time he preached for thirty years. Then he was converted to preaching without notes. He told me that it was the greatest thing that ever happened to his ministry. Why? Preaching without notes gives you a wonderful freedom to connect with your congregation. It also gives you authority.

Let me share my own experience. I followed an outstanding preacher in one of my first appointments. His name was Ron Ingram. The town was a lovely community called Norris, about 30 miles outside Knoxville. The Methodist Church was the liveliest place in town when I got there. A beautiful new sanctuary and a large, active group of young families were testimony to Ron's effectiveness. I was very young and insecure. I was even more so when people told me about my predecessor's preaching. "Oh, Ron Ingram is a wonderful preacher," they said. "He's the best I've ever heard." And here was the clincher, "And he never takes a note into the pulpit."

I turned pale the first time anybody said that to me. I had always written out my messages word-for-word and I had read them word-for-word. They were going to crucify me. I was going to be martyred--impaled on the spire of the new gleaming sanctuary.

I went home and I worked like a dog. When Sunday came I knew that sermon backwards and forwards and upside down. Bravely I mounted the pulpit, no notes--not a one. I proceeded to preach for at least an hour. Without notes I couldn't find a place to stop. I'm not the only one that has happened to. But people were reasonably complimentary. I wasn't Ron Ingram, but they knew my heart was in it. The next week I got it down to 30 minutes. Soon I was able to come to a halt in about twenty minutes, and people were really saying nice things! I was hooked--and I've never gone back. Neither will you if you give it a real try.

Gordon Clinard, professor of Preaching at Southwestern Baptist Theological Seminary, said, "Can you imagine our Lord standing on the Mountain saying 'Blessed are the . . . uh . . . uh . . . uh . . .'" and having to look at his notes?"

Of course, preaching without notes forces you to be simple, which I believe on its own is an asset. C. S. Lewis once declared that an articulation of the gospel that is both substantive and intelligible to a six-year-old should be required of any candidate for ordination. Albert Einstein once said, "You don't really understand something unless you can communicate it in a simple way." The songwriter was right when he wrote, "It's a gift to be simple . . ."

Preaching without notes allows you to read your congregation instead of your notes. It allows you to be personal. The advantages simply cannot be overstated.

E. Stanley Jones, a Wesleyan Methodist preacher and missionary, told of his first experience in preaching. He had studied to be a lawyer, and the first sermon he ever preached was a tremendous brief, or argument, for Christ. He presented all the logic and all the reasons, but, as he came to the end of the sermon, he realized how cold it was. And he closed the sermon saying, "I have delivered my sermon, now let me tell you what Christ has done for me." He proceeded to give his testimony, and it broke the ice. People began to respond. He wrote that from that point on in his ministry, he determined that God had called him to simply witness to what he had experienced, not argue the case on God's behalf. [30]

Preaching without notes gives the opportunity to seem more spontaneous. Judy Garland used to do a bit where she pretended to have forgotten the words of the song she was singing. While she seemed to be teetering on the edge of disaster, trying to remember, the audience held its breath, convinced they were seeing something truly special. Judy had that audience in the palm of her hand.

Preaching without notes is not preaching without preparation. Preparation is still essential. One of the greatest speakers of our time, Winston Churchill, wore out part of the carpet in front of a full-length mirror in his home. "That," pointed out the guide, "is where the Prime Minister practiced his extemporaneous speeches."

Many Las Vegas headliners are masters at convincing every audience that they're seeing a unique performance—that the entertainer is really "on" that night. The illusion of spontaneity sells his or her performance. It may seem effortless, but it doesn't happen by accident. The best performers rehearse routines that make every audience feel special. [31]

You may be wedded to a manuscript and there is no way that I can convince you to give it up. And, yes, there are some fine manuscript preachers. Let me at least make a couple of suggestions.

If you write out your message, make it as informal–as conversational as possible. One speech expert suggests you write in fragments. Take a look at this example that I took from a business publication: "Our customer evaluates us at a glance. A snapshot. Good bad. Pass fail. If it's exciting. Interesting. Challenging. And, yes, even fun. Are there risks? Uncertainties? Dangers? Sure. You bet. Competition is often chaotic and unpredictable."

If you are going to use a manuscript, study the style of Peter Marshall. Marshall's genius was his ability to write in an oral style and to deliver it in a dramatic way. If you can do that, I certainly won't argue with using a manuscript. Nevertheless, I would suggest that, as much as reasonably possible, you learn to preach without notes. Research shows that in a small church using notes does not impede communication. However, the larger the congregation, the more communication is impaired by notes.

In my own tradition, United Methodist, we like to tell the story of John Wesley's heart-warming experience at Aldersgate. Wesley had his life-changing experience while someone was reading the preface to Martin Luther's commentary on Romans.

I have a copy of that commentary on Romans. I've read that preface and I can't imagine anybody having a heart-warming experience while somebody was reading it aloud. However, note this, there were probably only a few people present that night at Aldersgate. And those listeners were more orally oriented than we are. They weren't used to watching television. So, as these words from Martin Luther were being read to those few people, probably everyone there was listening intently. Certainly John Wesley was. If there had been 200 people present that night or more, then those words might not have had the impact that they did. Wesley would probably not have had his heart-warming experience and there would be no Methodist church, no Nazarene church, no Holiness movement.

If you're a Baptist, you may be thinking, "Well, amen to that." But think through the implications of the research. If you have the opportunity to preach to a large congregation, try as much as possible to wean yourself from your notes.

I heard Norman Vincent Peale shortly before his death. I think he was 93 or 94 years of age at that time. He spoke to a National Speakers Association in Orlando. The amazing thing is he preached an entirely new message at 93 or 94 years of age. I know it was a new sermon because he included illustrations from changes that were taking place in the Soviet Union at just that moment. It was a terrific message. In fact, at the end, after preaching for an hour, Norman Vincent Peale received a standing ovation. It wasn't because of his age that he got the ovation. He got the ovation because it was a terrific message.

Norman Vincent Peale didn't look down a single time during that message. He didn't have any notes that I could see. He did stumble once. He forgot somebody's name. Now, I've stumbled over people's names for the past 20 years. I don't know what I'll do at 93. But that just made Peale seem more human when he stumbled.

But here's how he captivated his audience for one hour without notes. In the body of his message he told 3 powerful stories with just a little bit of verbiage in between. He had a powerful story for the opening and a powerful story for the closing. And it was wonderful. Can you really improve on his method? Anybody can remember 5 stories with a little preparation.

Preaching without notes is not a difficult task. You just have to dive in and do it. But I don't think anyone can do it well unless they've learned to illustrate.

If you cannot eliminate your notes, at least try to get by with a detailed outline. If you do use an outline, make it as oral as possible. Use short, choppy sentences and short, choppy paragraphs. Placidly reading a formal manuscript before a congregation is not preaching. It may be scholarly, it may be refined, it may be well-intended, but if it does not seek to involve or engage the congregation, it is not preaching. This is not to say that you can't preach from a manuscript. Some of our finest preachers do it that way. It is to say, however, that preaching is not reading, and your manuscript must be prepared as an oral presentation.

That is one reason African-American preaching is so appealing. Black preachers recognize the oral nature of preaching. White preaching often concentrates on the intellectual content being communicated. A great black preacher is aware of the content, of course, but he or she is also conscious of the timbre of his voice, the cadence of her sentences, the repetition of key phrases. That can be captured in a manuscript, but not without work.

Illustrations help us anchor ideas. As we've already noted, advertisers know that every important word in our vocabulary is anchored to a feeling. If I say to you "home," you have a feeling about that word. If I say "flag," a feeling. Even if I say "automobile," you may have a visceral response. If I say nearly any word that's important in our lives, there is an emotion that is anchored to that object.

Advertisers today are very sophisticated in anchoring images in our subconscious. They don't try to tell us all the advantages of their product. They don't have time in a 30-second spot or a 60-second spot. They try to anchor their product to a feeling.

For example, I remember when the Infiniti automobile first came out. The people who designed the ads didn't even show the Infiniti in their television spots. All they showed was the wind rustling in the trees when an Infiniti passed by. They wanted us to experience vicariously what it was like to drive an Infiniti. They didn't try to say that an Infiniti is better than a Lexus or a Rolls-Royce or a

Mercedes or a Cadillac. They just wanted to catch us up in the experience.

I got interested in this anchoring phenomenon some years back when the Timex watch company ran a series of ads. These ads, primarily in magazines, featured a full-page picture of a person. Down in the corner of the ad there was a small box containing text, saying something about that person.

My favorite was a picture of a man. The caption read like this, "Edwin Robinson became blind and deaf after a truck accident. Nine years later, he was struck by lightning and within hours his vision and hearing were restored. Edwin is wearing a Timex."

Now, what in the world has wearing a Timex got to do with being struck by lightning and having your hearing and your sight restored? Not a thing. They don't even say he was wearing a Timex at the time. All they're trying to do is anchor in our minds the idea that if he had been wearing a Timex, "It takes a licking and . . ." What? ". . . keeps on ticking." That's anchoring. Illustration is how we anchor ideas in a sermon.

I want to let one of my favorite preachers sum up this chapter on the art of sermon illustration. In the *Handbook of Contemporary Preaching* (Broadman & Holman), Steve Brown has a chapter on "Illustrating the Sermon" in which he makes this observation: "Let me give you a principle: If you can't illustrate it, don't preach it. By that principle, I do not mean that every point must have an illustration, or that without illustration, God cannot use the preaching of His Word. However, by that I do mean that if you cannot think of an illustration—a person, a story, a situation to which to apply the truth—then the truth is at best irrelevant or at worst simply not true. Truth that does not apply to real life is not worth preaching." Amen, Brother Steve.

Four Levels of Illustrations

We've looked at many reasons why we illustrate. Now let's consider four levels of illustrations. I took this concept from Haddon Robinson and I want to give him credit. Understanding these four levels was so helpful to me that I thought they might be helpful to you as well. They're very simple and they should be obvious. But if you don't think through these four levels of illustrations, you may not be as effective in your preaching as you would like to be.

Level one, something I have read but could not have experienced. Now think for just a moment of an example of this kind of illustration. "Something I have read but could not have experienced." For example, how about the classics—Shakespeare, Milton, Keats?

I have a friend who is known as a classical preacher. He has a vast library. He's very well read. Most of his illustrations come from the classics, from Shakespeare, Dante, and so on. He's very articulate and he preaches very eloquent sermons. However, his church is declining. And if he were to ask my advice—which he never will, by the way—but if he ever did, I would suggest to him that part of the problem might be his choice of illustrations.

I'm not saying you shouldn't quote from the classics. Many pastors do so from time to time and they add beauty to their messages. However, if your primary source of illustrations is something you have read but could not have experienced, you're not going to touch very many lives.

Level two, something I have experienced but my congregation has not experienced. Now this is better, I can get excited about something that I personally have experienced. Sometimes hobbies fall into this category. If you're a golfer or if you grow roses or if you have grandchildren or any other significant interests, you will probably draw some interesting material from these interests. That's fine as long as you don't overdo it. It's better than simply sharing something you've only read about and to which hardly anyone can relate.

Level three is something I have read or heard but my congregation has experienced. Now this is better. This is much better.

I served two small rural churches while I was going to seminary. Most of my flock were dairy farmers. I'd never been on a farm in my life. I grew up in the suburbs. I've never milked a cow, never slopped a pig or whatever you do with pigs. I don't know anything about farming. But my congregation was made up of farm families. I would try to relate to their experience. I'd try to find an illustration out of rural life.

For example, I heard Dr. Robert Schuller tell a story years ago. It came out of his growing-up years in the Midwest. It was about a group of farmers who grew potatoes. Each Saturday, they would load up their pickup trucks with these potatoes and haul them off to market. But before they could take the potatoes to market, it was necessary for them to sort the potatoes and put the small potatoes on the bottom and the medium-sized potatoes in the middle and the large potatoes on top. They were paid according to the size of their potatoes. They received the most for the large potatoes and got the least for the small potatoes. And if you didn't sort out your potatoes before you took them to market, the man at the market paid you as if they were all small potatoes. So it was really important to sort those potatoes before going to market and all the farmers did . . . except one.

There was one farmer who never sorted his potatoes before he took them to the market. He would leave home with them unsorted. Later, he presented his potatoes to the man who ran the market. All the other farmers talked about this man, how irresponsible he was. They knew he was getting paid as though all his potatoes were small potatoes. "That's what he deserves," they said, "since he's too lazy to sort his potatoes."

Until one day, one of the farmers overheard the man who ran the market paying this man who never sorted his potatoes, and lo and behold, the man who ran the market was paying this man the same amount he was paying everybody else. This is starting to sound like a parable of Jesus, isn't it? Well, this caused an uproar. This lazy farmer was being paid the same amount as everybody who went to all that trouble sorting their potatoes. So the farmers went *en masse* and confronted the man who ran the market and said, "Look, we know that lazy fellow does not sort his potatoes before he brings them to market, and yet we understand you're paying him the same amount as you're paying us. It's not fair."

And the man who ran the market said, "Oh? But he does sort his potatoes before he brings them to market. It's true he doesn't sort them before he leaves home. But he deliberately drives to market on one of the roughest roads in the county, and as he bounces along in his pickup truck the potatoes start moving around and the small potatoes naturally gravitate to the bottom, and the middle sized potatoes gravitate to the middle, and the large potatoes rise to the top."

Schuller's title for his sermon, by the way, was "Large Potatoes Rise to the Top on a Rough and Rocky Road." If you're familiar with Dr. Schuller's theology, you can see how appropriate this story would be.

Now, if I were preaching in those two little country churches today, I might tell that story. I would preface it by saying that I heard this on Dr. Robert Schuller's show. And I would further admit that I don't know if potatoes will move around in a truck like that or not, but that's how the story goes. They could give me feedback after the service about whether something like that could actually happen. Telling that story that relates to their experience is better than telling a story out of my experience to which they might not be able to relate.

And this brings us to the fourth level. And you can probably guess what it is. *Something I have experienced and something the congregation has experienced.* The whole purpose of this exercise is to impress upon you that the best kind of illustration is something out of our common experience, something with which everyone can relate.

Wasn't that Jesus' method? He used common everyday items—plants, birds, seeds—to impress truth upon people. He talked about things straight out of the headlines—an ancient tower in Siloam in south Jerusalem which fell, killing 18 people, and about some Galileans whose blood Pilate mixed with the sacrifices that were offered to pagan gods. Karl Barth's admonition to preach with a Bible in one hand and a newspaper in the other would fit Jesus' method of teaching hand-in-glove.

One January, Selina and I were doing seminars in Florida. [It's a rough life but somebody's got to do it.] We had a seminar scheduled in Miami on a Monday. We left Knoxville early on a Saturday morning to get there. We drove because we had a ton of books and tapes we would be selling in the seminar. But we were having car trouble so we left early and kept driving the entire distance. We drove until late Saturday night and made it to Fort Lauderdale just north of Miami. We decided that since it was Saturday night and we had Sunday to rest and get ready for the seminar, we would stay in a motel on Fort Lauderdale beach.

When I'm near a beach, I like to get up early in the morning and take long walks on the beach. We had some time before we needed to get ready for church and so I did just that. I put on some old clothes and started walking on the Fort Lauderdale beach. I had a two day growth of beard because I was worried about the car and had left early Saturday morning without shaving.

So there I was looking somewhat unkempt, unshaven, with my old clothes on walking down the beach. I passed a couple of guys going the same direction I was, just not as quickly. They looked like they might be homeless. They weren't walking together. They were walking singularly. But they were both headed in the same direction. They had on old clothes. They were unshaven. I thought to myself, I wonder if there's a shelter they're going to early on a Sunday morning to get breakfast? I didn't think much more about it, but I kept walking until I got down to the Fort Lauderdale marina. It was on my right; the ocean was on my left.

I gazed somewhat longingly at all the magnificent yachts in the Fort Lauderdale marina. Then I noticed on the other side of the street from the marina was a park alongside the beach. This is where the homeless men were headed. There was a large gathering of homeless people there. But right in the middle of all the homeless people, there were also 35 or 40 men and women. They were all clean-shaven and nicely dressed. And you know what they were doing? They were fixing breakfast. They all had picnic baskets and coolers, and they had made little signs and put them around the park. The signs were in pairs. One sign said, "Jesus loves you," and the other sign said, "Just as you are." And these clean shaven, nicely dressed people were preparing breakfast for the homeless. I felt a little doxology within my heart. I was so proud of them for being there.

Well, I hadn't shaved, and I had my old clothes on, and breakfast looked so good that I . . . No, I didn't really. But a few weeks later, my pastor asked me to fill in for him one Sunday morning. We have a large church with a large number of affluent young families. And I thought we needed a mission sermon. It had been a while. And so, I started off telling about this group of church people who took their Sunday mornings to feed the homeless. You see, everybody can relate to that. Everybody's been on a beach at one time or another. Everyone has seen homeless people. It was something that just about anybody could relate to. It's not rocket science. That is your best kind of illustration, and if you can add a little humor to the situation, it's going to make it that much more effective.

You may be thinking, "King, that's so obvious." Is it? My friend who's a classical preacher, it's not obvious to him. It would change his whole ministry if it were obvious to him. You see what I'm saying? Examine the illustrations you are using. Level four illustrations are the kind Jesus used.

Finding Exciting Sermon Illustrations

It is said that English author William Makepeace Thackeray always tipped his hat whenever he passed the house in which he wrote *Vanity Fair*. I feel that way when I come across a really good sermon illustration. It is indeed a pearl of great price, treasure hidden in the field.

Where do we find illustrations? No less a preacher than Harry Emerson Fosdick once said that finding good illustrations was the hardest thing he did. Fosdick was one who was often accused in his later years of using too many illustrations. It is said that when he went back and edited some of his earlier works, he invariably added more illustrations. He believed in illustrations.

Where do we find illustrations? Everywhere! Good preaching is ultimately good conversation. What makes good conversation? Gossip? A good story? Something humorous that happened to you? Remember this, if it's a great story at the supermarket, it'll probably be a great story in the pulpit.

Good preaching is good conversation. Unless, of course, you are in a very authoritarian church where you can say to folks, "Jump," and they ask antiphonally, "How high, how high, how high?" Unless you're in that kind of church, in order to really affect, help, comfort and counsel the people in your congregation, you've got to talk from the pulpit as if you were speaking to them one-on-one. You don't preach to a congregation; you talk to individuals within the congregation. And you do it in a conversational style, and you look for illustrations that make for good conversation.

There was a story in the newspapers a few years ago about a census worker who was afraid of dogs. She came to a house surrounded by a tall fence. She thought, "Uh-oh! I bet that means they've got a dog." So she looked all over the yard. She didn't see a dog so she very quietly opened the gate, then closed it behind her. She crept up to the front door. She dreaded knocking on the door just in case there was still a dog somewhere in the yard that she hadn't spotted—perhaps at the back of the house, or perhaps even inside the house. She knocked very quietly.

Fortunately, the lady of the house came to the door. She was alone. No dog. Then the lady of the house bit the census worker.

That actually happened. The lady of the house bit the census worker on the arm. She had to be treated at the hospital for a human bite which, as you may know, can be worse than a dog bite. If I were preaching a sermon on the unpredictability of human nature, how you could predict what an animal is going to do better than you can predict what a human being is going to do, that would be a good story. Straight out of the newspapers. Everybody can relate to it. It's a little bit quirky. It gets everybody's attention. As far as I'm concerned, if it makes good conversation, it makes good preaching.

I was on the road one time and I heard broadcaster Paul Harvey tell about a new diet that baseball manager Tommy Lasorda was trying to follow. He did wonderfully well for a while on that diet. In fact, he made television commercials praising that diet. But he now was struggling.

Tommy Lasorda said, "I am a strong man, but linguine is stronger." And I thought, that'll preach. Samson was a strong man, but his lust for Delilah was stronger . . . Saul was a strong man, but his jealousy of David was stronger . . . Pilate was one of the most powerful men of his time, but his fear of popular opinion was stronger, and so on . . . You get the idea.

As I was preparing the materials for one workshop, there was an article about President George H. W. Bush removing his shoes before meeting with the president of South Korea for a meal. Several of President Bush's top aides were with him including his Secretary of State, James Baker. All of them left their shoes carefully arranged outside the door when they went in to eat with the South Korean president.

Finding Exciting Sermon Illustrations

You know how government bureaucrats are—all the shoes looked exactly the same. Some helpful worker in the government palace came along and moved the shoes while the delegation was meeting with the South Korean president, then re-arranged the shoes elsewhere in the hallway. Imagine the scene. The president of the most powerful nation on earth and several of his top aides hopping around the presidential palace in South Korea trying to match up shoes with feet. Fortunately, I just happened to be working on a sermon for *Dynamic Preaching* on Jesus washing the feet of his disciples. I could begin with an illustration of a custom in one part of the world, removing your shoes before you eat, and tie it to the tradition of washing feet in Jesus' time.

Mass media, magazines, newspapers, and of course, today the Internet are all good sources of illustrations. Of course, if you take your illustrations from printed material, it helps if you learn how to cough loudly. You don't know about the cough method of researching sermon illustrations? You're sitting in your doctor's office reading a magazine and you run across a great illustration and … [cough—rip!!] . . . That joke works better live, obviously.

I'm not really recommending that you tear pages out of other people's magazines. But illustrations are everywhere. Of course, the Internet takes away any excuse today for not finding exciting illustrative material.

Our primary source of illustrations is our personal experiences. Our secondary source for great illustrations is the mass media. Now, why didn't I say the great theologians? Theologians don't illustrate. That's one of the problems with theology. Mass media is where we find the stories to which people relate. That was Jesus' method, as we've already noted. I don't ever recall Jesus ever saying, "Well, as Gamaliel says . . ." —Gamaliel being the leading authority of his day. Follow Jesus' example. Use current events and common everyday items.

We have a little column in our newspaper called "25 Years Ago." It's about interesting things that happened 25 years ago. There was a column about a Church of God somewhere that had contracted with a big moving company to move their church. The moving company literally picked the church off its foundation and moved it across town. It was a little white-framed church, obviously. But somehow, the moving company got mixed up and moved a nearby church, a Church of Christ by mistake. So here comes this pastor down the street and there's his church, much to his surprise, the Church of Christ, coming to meet him. To me, that's a great sermon illustration. We all want to get our church moving. Look for fun, quirky stories like that one and you will keep people awake.

Now, the final source of illustrations is your own congregation. There are two ways in which that's true. Every once in a while, I run into a pastor who has lay people in his or her congregation collect illustrations in his or her behalf. That's a great idea. What happens when you use one of the stories that someone has collected in your behalf? They sit up a little taller and they listen a little more intently, and they have a warm feeling toward their pastor. Explain to your people why you use stories in your preaching, how you're trying to translate the truth of God into everyday life and enlist their help in finding great material.

But there's another way in which people in your congregation can help you collect great illustrations. Everybody has a story to tell. Back when I was a young pastor, I didn't like to visit. I don't know about you, but I'm an introvert. I'm much more comfortable with my nose buried in a book than I am with people. One reason I didn't like to visit was that I didn't really know why I was doing it. Was I just making a social call, a sales call, what? I'm not a person who can deal with a lot of ambiguity. I like to know exactly why I'm there and what I'm supposed to be doing, and nobody ever helped me understand what pastoral visitation is all about.

If I were doing it all over again, I would spend more time doing visitation and I would enjoy it more because I would be asking people to tell me their stories. Some of those stories, I would be able to tell later on. I'm not talking about breaking confidences. You never do that. Some stories cannot be told for 20 years and 2000 miles later. Some of them can never be told. Some of the names will have to be changed; the locale will have to be changed, and so on. You don't break confidences. At the same time, you're going to be hearing stories from time to time that will grace your ministry for many, many years.

I used to buy lots of books. My goal was to come up with 200 new illustrations each month to keep *Dynamic Preaching* fresh and vital. I would often buy used books or remainders of hardbacks that had just gone to paperback. I would buy them cheap and tear them up. I didn't have time to write everything down or even to make copies. I would literally tear the pages out of the books and file those pages by subject matter. That mortified my family. They felt that books are somehow sacred. It was embarrassing when I borrowed a book from the library and absentmindedly tore out some pages. Now I download things to my Kindle and roam the Internet. The modern world is so wonderful.

Popular books are a good source of illustrations, as are business books, self-help books, biographies. George Buttrick used to tell his students to read a book every week. Of course, you probably do that already. I run into pastors who haven't read a new book since they graduated from seminary. That's sad. You need to keep growing. You need to keep stimulating those little gray cells that Hercule Poirot talks about. Read the theologians, read church history, etc., but for illustration purposes—read newspapers, magazines, radio, television, popular books. I like popular religious authors like Max Lucado, Steve Brown, Chuck Swindoll, John Ortberg. The very best collection of sermon illustrations ever printed is Fred Craddock's *Craddock Stories* (St. Louis: Chalice Press, 2001). Order it today from Amazon. And, of course, I must put a plug in for *Dynamic Preaching* available online at Sermons.com or in print form by calling 1-800-848-5547.

Don't forget cartoon and humor books. Abraham Lincoln kept a humor book in a desk drawer in his office and read jokes to his staff every day during the Civil War. He said it helped him survive psychologically. Pastors can also be under much stress. It would help if you'd take a humor break every day. It would also be a good source of illustrations.

The best stories, however, are drawn from your own experience. I say that in spite of the fact that over the past quarter of a century through *Dynamic Preaching* we probably have supplied more pastors with more good stories than anybody in the country. I don't apologize for that. Most pastors simply don't have the time to collect all the material needed to preach every Sunday. Some pastors still preach 3 times a week. How do you do that?

Nevertheless, the best illustrations are drawn from your own experiences. The question is, how do we go about collecting such material? I want to deal for a moment with the question of how to go about collecting personal illustrations.

You begin by developing what can only be called a "homiletical eye." That is, you discipline yourself to constantly search for sermon fodder in the everyday events of life.

A friend of mine who is now with the Lord, Jerry Anderson, was a genius at this. Jerry was my pastor for many years. Jerry was a student of nature. He was also a student of people. One day, I was in his study while he was watching a cowbird laying an egg in a wren's nest outside his study window. As a student of nature, he knew that cowbirds do this. They'll lay their eggs in another bird's nest and when the cowbird eggs hatch, the baby cowbird will be larger than the other chicks in the nest and, eventually, the baby cowbird will starve out the other baby birds.

Jerry watched later in the spring as this large baby cowbird was being frantically fed by a much smaller wren. He watched as this mother wren flew frantically all over the church yard trying to get enough food to keep that baby cowbird happy. Jerry turned to me and he said, "Isn't that like a lot of folks in the church who want the lion's share of the pastor's attention?"

Now of course, he wouldn't use that in a sermon for obvious reasons. But it was the kind of observation he was continually making, and most of his observations could be applied to the pulpit. Discipline yourself to look daily for events that could be used in the pulpit. They're out there, but you have to look for them.

I stopped at a Burger King several years back. I was in a self-destructive mood, so I decided to order a Whopper. I went up to the counter and there was a very young woman behind the counter, a teeny-bopper really, maybe 16 or 17 years old. I said "I want a Whopper, minus onion, and a small diet coke."

She hit the keys on the register and said "That'll be $1.34." (That should give you a hint how long ago this was.)

I said, "That's too cheap. It's got to be more than that."

She said, "No, that's right. It'll be $1.34."

I said, "Something's going on." The Whopper was $.99 (I was surprised at that), and the diet coke was $.70, and I said "There's no way they could amount to $1.34."

She said "That's right. It's $1.34."

So I said "Fine." I paid her the $1.34. I'm standing there studying that sign. There's an older woman standing beside the counter, a Burger King employee, and I turned to her and said, "You know, that can't be right."

She said "Well, I'll tell you what happened." She says, "We have on our cash register a button we call 'the assume button.' If the person behind the counter thinks that the customer might qualify for a senior citizen discount, but doesn't want to ask, they can go ahead and hit that assume button and give them the discount."

That broke me of eating Whoppers. Me, a senior? But of course I couldn't help but think, "I wonder how many of us walk around with "assume buttons." We hear somebody who talks differently than we do, or we see somebody who looks different, and that hits our "assume button." A person could use that in a sermon sometime if they were so inclined.

You know the name Robert Fulghum. Fulghum wrote a little book, *Everything I Needed to Know I Learned in Kindergarten*. It was the number one best-selling book in America some few years back. He followed with another best seller-based on an old joke, *It Was on Fire When I Lay Down on It*. Then there was, *Uh-uh!* and *Maybe (Maybe Not)*. I don't know how many books Robert Fulghum has written or how many he's sold. Millions, I'm sure.

Fulghum is a retired Unitarian pastor. Those books are simply collections of stories out of his own experience. You could write a book like Robert Fulghum. Pastors have an amazing variety of experiences. Frederick Buechner once said that it would help us all if we would keep track of the times and events in our lives that bring tears to our eyes. Anybody who works with people has interesting things happen all the time. Just think of the funny things that have happened at weddings and funerals.

I'll never forget in Maryland when I was a student pastor, they put the minister in the lead car in the procession to drive to the cemetery after the funeral. I'm rather absent-minded, I drive on remote control as it were. And they put me in the lead car.

Well, I'm driving along and I pass a drive-in restaurant where I sometimes stopped for coffee. Absentmindedly, I pulled into the parking lot of that little drive-in, forgetting I had all these cars following me. When I happened to look back and saw them, I drove right on through the parking lot and back onto the main road and the entire procession followed right behind me as if nothing had happened. It took a long time to live that down. Of course 5 years later, it was funny. [I first told that story, which actually happened, 40 years ago. It's amazing how many pastors since have claimed that story as their own.] Who hasn't done dumb things? They happen all the time, and those are your best illustrations. People relate to those experiences and those experiences endear you to them.

Now there are some important steps you need to take to become a great user of personal illustrations. First of all, you're going to have to spend some time observing and reflecting about your experiences. Observe the things that are happening around you and write them down immediately. Make detailed notes. Carry an iPad, a notebook, a voice recorder or some means of collecting these fascinating incidents. Then at the end of the day, look over these interesting incidents that have occurred and put them in a file. This is the secret of some of the most effective communicators in this land. They write everything down. Don't depend on your memory. I don't care how great the story was, you will forget.

The King of Hearts, in *Through the Looking Glass* declares, "The horror of that moment I shall never, never forget."

The queen replies, "You will though, if you don't make a memorandum of it."

A reporter went to Samuel Clemens' hometown and an old man said to him, "Well, I knew as many stories as Sam Clemens ever knew. The only difference is he wrote them down and I didn't." And that is the difference, my friend. Start making notes, detailed notes, not just one word. I have so many slips of paper in my desk that say something like "Volkswagen" on it. Something interesting obviously happened to me some time that involved a Volkswagen, but I look at that piece of paper now and I have no idea what it refers to. You've got to make detailed notes on what happened and your feelings at the time because the feelings are what make the story. If you get in the habit of doing that, it will make a wonderful resource. It will be something you can give your grandchildren someday, if you do not write a book and give it to posterity.

Use illustrations that reveal your vulnerability. Nothing will turn your people off quicker than an illustration that could be interpreted as bragging. People will respond most surely if you share your weaknesses and not your strengths. If you do something embarrassing, fall on your face, commit a *faux pas*, share it with your people. As you share your struggles and share how God helped you through those struggles, then you will find that your lay people can relate to those experiences and that will give them hope. It will also give them a warm feeling toward their pastor. However, remember that personal illustrations require authenticity.

I didn't really think much about this until I was reading C.S. Lewis some time back. Lewis was telling about visiting a church. In the process of giving his message, the pastor used a throwaway line that went something like this, "Our home life must be the foundation of our natural life." C.S. Lewis said he looked around the church and people were hanging their heads in embarrassment all over that church because they knew that pastor's home life and they knew that he didn't really mean what he was saying.

In one of her books, Barbara Johnson tells about a cartoon she saw in which a man was standing on a street corner. Passersby were hurrying around him. He was throwing a tantrum, while saying, "Doesn't anybody want to know the source of my inner peace?" You've got to be credible. Nothing is hidden. People know when you're not genuine in the pulpit.

Let people share in your struggle of faith. My friend, Jerry, cried all afternoon after the doctors diagnosed his wife as having inoperable lung cancer. She wasn't a smoker. It just happened. When he got the news, he said all he could do was cry and pray, "Please, God, have mercy." In fact, he began to hurt so much that he found himself unable to pray. He shared this experience with our congregation. Many of those present came up to him following the service and responded that in times of great hurt, they found themselves unable to pray, too. Obviously, Jerry was not urging people to forsake prayer. He was sharing about the depth of his despair and when he did, people connected. Your lay people need to know about your struggles because they are struggling with some of the same issues.

Look for humor in human weakness. The last part of this book will deal with using humor from the pulpit. But I want you to think about humor in a broader sense here. Humor comes from the same root word as does humility and *humus*, dirt. We live in a funny world. All humor grows out of human weakness.

You won't find much in the work of great theologians on humor. Theologians are humorless people, my observation is (though I will confess that Will Willimon is somewhat of a theologian, and he has a wonderful wit). Personally I'd be laughing all the time if I called myself a theologian. The study of God. That's funny. I visualize ants studying human beings. Karl Barth does have a little section on humor in his work on grace and that's where humor belongs. Humor reminds us that we are fallible.

Mark Twain once said there'll be no humor in heaven. Why? He wasn't saying there wouldn't be any joy in heaven. He said there won't be any humor. Because all humor is based on human weakness. And that weakness reminds us that we are dependent on God. Humor is a reminder of the grace of God.

Dr. Doug Adams speaks on humor in the Bible. He has a beautiful analogy that he employs. He would have us hold two images in mind. The first image is that of a magician. The key to being a good magician is to do everything perfectly. That's the only way your tricks will work. The magician comes out dressed in a tuxedo, every hair's in place. He is tall, confident and poised. He has his beautiful assistant with him. The magician does his tricks, and we ooh and aah and sit there like little children. That's one image.

The second image is the clown. The clown is the antithesis of the magician. The clown dresses in baggy pants and shoes that are way too large. He bends over to pick something up and somebody whacks him on the behind. Everything the clown does is wrong.

Doug Adams says Biblical characters are more like clowns than magicians. Look at the heroes of the Bible. Abraham, the father of our faith, passes off Sarah his wife as his sister. He's a coward. Abraham didn't always "walk by faith." So you tell the whole story of Abraham, and what you have is grace. You're able to say, "Look, these men and women were just like we are. Anything they accomplished, they did it by the grace of God." [32]

When I graduated from the seminary and went into my first pastorate, I wanted everybody to see me as a magician. Can you relate to that? I wanted to do everything perfectly and have everybody ooh and aah. "Look at the things King Duncan can do." It took me a lot of maturity before I realized I really helped people more if they saw me as a clown. They needed to see that anything I accomplished was only by the grace of God. The most effective pastors I know are not afraid to be vulnerable, not afraid to show their weakness.

Maintain your integrity in your choice of illustrations. Howard Hughes, in his Hollywood days, was busy producing a historical epic. A newly hired assistant pointed out that there was a particular scene that was somewhat ludicrous because of a historical inaccuracy. When the young man suggested to Hughes that he should go to the library and check out the historicity of this particular scene, Hughes shouted at him, "Never check an interesting historical fact." Some preachers seem to follow that same philosophy. Eventually, it catches up with you and hurts your witness.

Don't force it if it doesn't fit. We've all done it, I suspect. We've run across a great story that we just can't wait to tell. I mean, it's so good we just can't resist, and so we force it on into a sermon where it doesn't belong.

It's like the preacher who came across the character in the gospels called, Simon the Leaper. He imagined all sorts of things that this Leaper character might have done, leaping from mountain to mountain, hill to hill. He preached a sermon on Simon the Leaper. Then someone brought to his attention that the man's name was Simon the Leper . . . to which the preacher replied, "I don't see the need to throw away a good sermon illustration just because of a difference in pronunciation."

A good story is priceless. But if it doesn't help your sermon, leave it in your files. Maybe you will find a use for it later. A gratuitous illustration that does not belong, no matter how great a story, will ultimately rob your sermon of its natural power.

If your illustrations come from a particular interest that you have, make sure everybody can relate. For example, if you're a golfer, it's all right to include a modest number of golfing stories from time to time. Don't overdo it, and please make sure that you don't use jargon that only golfers can understand. You'll turn off the rest of your congregation completely. If you're serving a blue-collar congregation, there may not be many of them who play golf or play tennis. You may want to keep such illustrations to a minimum.

I had a friend who grew orchids. He was always talking about orchids in his messages. There aren't many orchid growers in our part of the country. Make sure your folks can identify with your experiences.

Plan your preaching a year in advance. I'm only half-way kidding. Planning in advance allows you to look ahead to when a particular story will be appropriate. Many pastors use vacation time for this. Don't. That's unfair to your spouse. You ought to be able to legitimately ask your church to allow you a special time to get away for this purpose in a setting away from pressure, where your creative juices can flow. Then as you collect illustrations, you will see times and places where they can be used with maximum effectiveness.

If you can't plan a year ahead, at least plan six weeks ahead, or three weeks at a minimum. The late Louis L'Amour, prolific writer of western novels, had as many as six books in progress at the same time. This allowed him to take full advantage of his research efforts. When he found facts or discovered ideas not applicable to the story on which he was working, he could use the information in another story also in progress. This method allowed him to produce hundreds of novels.

Even if you can't plan a year ahead, at least begin on next Sunday's sermon on Monday or Tuesday. It is amazing, if you plan ahead, how many illustrations will pop out at you. Saturday night is too late. Sunday morning is obviously worse.

Generally I prepare *Dynamic Preaching* sermons thirteen at a time. In that way if I run across a good story that won't fit one place, I can look ahead nine or ten weeks and see if it will fit there. That helps me get away from forcing illustrations where they don't belong. Even more importantly, if I know what I'm going to be preparing several weeks in advance, the subject will "percolate" in my subconscious. It's amazing how many illustrations, then, will jump out at me as I go through the weeks leading up to that time.

A church invited me to speak for their Stewardship Sunday. They were going to try to raise a million dollars in one day, and they invited me to speak for that service. The pastor chuckled as he said, "King, you've got to raise a million dollars in one service, but don't let that put any pressure on you."

To make matters worse, they gave me the title for my message. I hate for somebody to give me a title. For one thing, it means I can't go to the barrel and draw out something I've used before (truth in preaching). But the chief reason is that I like to do my own thing and have things come to me as they will (via the Holy Spirit, hopefully).

But they gave me the title, "Because We Care." That was the theme of their financial campaign. They said, "Now, 4 weeks from today, we need you to speak on this subject in our worship service. Then we'll take up the pledge cards." So I went through those 4 weeks leading up to that pledge campaign, and I had that theme percolating in my brain, and illustrations started jumping out at me during the weeks leading up to that service, but I couldn't come up with a conclusion for the message. I got all the way up to the Friday night before that Sunday and I still did not know how I was going to close that message.

I will never forget. I was staying at the Camaro Inn in Kingsport, Tennessee, where I was speaking through Saturday night. I checked into the hotel and went directly to my room. On a desk in the room I noticed there were some cards for their guests to fill out. Imagine my surprise when I read on the top of one of those cards, "Because we care." A cold chill went up my spine when I saw that. It was an evaluation card for me to indicate how well the Camaro Inn had served me.

When I got into the pulpit the following Sunday morning and got to the end of the message, I pulled out that little card from the Camaro Inn with the words "Because We Care." I explained how I happened to have it. I said that the Camaro Inn wanted me to tell them whether they cared enough about me as a customer. And then I said, "In a few moments you're going to be bringing cards to this altar that say, 'Because We Care.' As you do you will be indicating how much you care about the work of God in this church . . ."

You get the idea. Very simple. The point is, that card would not have jumped out at me if I had not been living with that theme for the preceding 4 weeks. If you wait until Saturday to choose your theme, such things are less apt to happen to you. This is the advantage of preaching a series of sermons. Perhaps you follow a lectionary and you already know what your text is going to be. Why not look ahead and plan your major themes several weeks in advance? It would make all the difference in the world for some pastors.

One pastor never prepared during the week, and on Sunday morning he'd sit on the platform while the church was singing the hymns, desperately praying, "Lord, give me your message, Lord give me your message."

One Sunday, while desperately praying for God's message, he heard the Lord say, "Ralph, here's my message. You're lazy!"

All illustrations, properly used, are helpful; personal illustrations, even more so. When we communicate at the point of our humanness, we give people hope. I am assuming, of course, that you do not break confidences or embarrass people in sharing personal experiences.

The theological progression is: the biblical story, my story, the people's story. Rhetorically, you might alter that progression. The posture of such preaching is, I don't have all the answers, but here's where I've been and here is what worked for me. As Frederick Buechner has so well stated it, "My assumption is that the story of anyone of us is in some measure the story of us all."

Add Drama to Your Preaching

"It ain't what you say, it's the way how you say it." That's a line from an old Louis Armstrong song, but it's true. Every student of communication will tell you that how you present your content is more important than the content itself. [What is that sound I hear? It's the sound of my old Homiletics professor turning over in his grave.]

Every great preacher through the ages has discovered ways to make his or her preaching more dramatic.

Be Passionate. Use your imagination for a moment. Imagine that you have a brand new car. You're proud of that car. It's a beauty. Now, imagine that, somehow, I find out where you live and I come to your house with a baseball bat and I pound that new car to smithereens.

You hear the noise and you come out. Then you run over to where I'm standing, exhausted by this time. Chances are, at that moment, you'll preach to me the best sermon you've ever preached.

That idea originated with speech consultant John Connellan. He often bets his business clients $50,000 that he can make them better public speakers in 10 seconds. This is the formula he uses.

Why do I say that this will be the best sermon you've ever preached? An effective sermon has three essential elements. You have something to say, you say it with clarity, and you say it with feeling. That's it. That's all it takes to have an effective sermon—something to say, say it clearly, say it with feeling. Obviously, it doesn't take a great intellect, a charismatic personality, a million dollar smile, or a Ph.D. beside your name to accomplish these three objectives. Anybody can do it. Then why is there so much poor preaching? Why do we hear so many sermons that violate one or all three of these essential elements?

John Ortberg tells of an interview he heard with a woman who runs the largest speakers' bureau in the world. The interviewer asked this woman, "What is the number one quality that makes someone an effective speaker?" Ortberg thought she would say intelligence or eloquence or charisma, but it was none of those. She said that the primary single quality that makes someone an effective speaker is passion. [33] That's true. I have heard sermons with many deficiencies that were heard gladly and with much effect because of the passion of the preacher.

For Soren Kierkegaard, the villain in Christianity was the theological professor who gathered information about the faith and lectured about the faith, but never caught the real thing. He perpetuated the idea that knowledge about Christianity is the same as Christianity.

Kierkegaard would have appreciated the whimsical story about the professor who was given the choice of two rooms, one where he could read about love and one where he could experience it. The professor chose the room where he could read about love.

David Hume, the skeptical Scottish philosopher and historian, regularly attended a church service conducted by a sternly orthodox minister. A friend once suggested to Hume that he was being inconsistent in going to listen to such a preacher.

Hume answered, "Look, I don't believe all my pastor says, but he does, and every once in a while I like to hear a man who believes what he says."

When an editor of the *London Times* asked Charles Spurgeon for permission to publish his sermons, the famous preacher said, "Go ahead, but you can't print my fire."

A young minister being interviewed by William Sangster admitted that he wasn't the kind of preacher who would set the Thames River on fire.

Sangster replied, "I'm not interested in knowing if you would set the Thames River on fire, what I want to know is this: if I picked you up by the scruff of the neck and dropped you in the Thames, would it sizzle?"

John Wesley once said that when he preached, he set himself on fire and people came to watch him burn.

Such passion cannot be faked! George Burns' famous statement was, "Above all, be sincere. Once you can fake that, you've got it made."

That won't wash in this instance. We are talking about passion that springs from a genuine love of the Gospel. It's so important. Remember, excitement is contagious; so is every other emotion the pastor is feeling. Of all the preacher's tools, passion is the most important.

Passion does not mean loud. Jonathan Edwards read his sermons and hardly spoke above a whisper, and yet his sermon "Sinners in the Hands of an Angry God" caused men to cringe in their pews and weep their way to the altar for salvation.

In the old paradigm, credibility came from credentials—your position in a church hierarchy—your education. Today credibility comes not from your credentials but from your commitment. As is so often said, people don't care how much you know until they know how much you care. They want to feel your passion when you are presenting the message of the Gospel.

Make it personal. A great cellist and conductor, Mstislav Rostropovich once said, "If you are playing for 18,000 people, play as if for one with 17,999 eavesdroppers."

Daniel Webster was a good judge of preachers and of preaching. He once said, "Many ministers take their texts from Paul and preach from the newspapers. When they do, I prefer to enjoy my own thoughts rather than to listen. If they would preach more to individuals and less to the crowds, there would not be so much complaint of the decline of true religion."

When you get into the pulpit, you ought to be thinking in terms of communicating one-on-one with everybody in the room. You're not preaching to a congregation; you're conversing with an individual person.

Speak clearly, distinctly, and slowly to grab undivided attention. Sandra Day O'Connor, the first woman to be named to the United States Supreme Court, is known for presenting herself this way. She has said that she trained herself to make people lean forward and pay attention if they wanted to hear what she had to say. 34

Charles E. Jeffers used to stand up in the pulpit and say to his congregation: "Today we're going to talk about what's on your mind and on mine." That was the way he began his message, and that's the way preaching ought to be directed. It is one reason every church ought to invest in a good sound system. Nothing is more personal than whispering into a microphone.

You may serve a small church. Folks will go off to hear a preacher at a conference or at some large church and they'll come back and say, "Oh That preacher was so wonderful. I felt like he was talking right to me." The reason they felt he was talking right to them was he's learned to make friends with his microphone, and nothing is more intense and more personal than that kind of communication. It's amazing to me, but I find some pastors today who are afraid of microphones. They won't make use of them. That's crazy in today's technological age.

Make friends with that mike and learn to use it to make your preaching as personal as possible. Is this manipulation? We used to worry excessively about such things when I was in seminary. Kierkegaard worried about such things too. "Have I the right to use my art to win over a person?" he asked. I personally believe there is a difference between effectively communicating your message and deliberately manipulating people for personal gain. I assume that none of you is a potential Jim Jones.

Part of being personal is reading your congregation while you are preaching. Nothing is more depressing than the preacher who never looks at his congregation, never acknowledges that they are there and that they are a vital part of the preaching event. Be personal.

Be creative. I love studying the old evangelists. Remember, they didn't have a built-in constituency. They had to find a way to draw a crowd. You and I can't get away with some of the things that the old-time evangelists did. I'm not talking about matters of personal behavior. No, I'm thinking of preachers like Billy Sunday. Billy was rough, sometimes even crude. When he was converted, Billy Sunday was a baseball player with the Chicago White Stockings. When God called him to preach, he had no education to speak of. He became a clerk at the YMCA in Chicago for a time before he started preaching.

When he began his ministry, he was quite unsophisticated. Many times, he would turn flips or do somersaults on the platform. He was known to rip books and break chairs. Sometimes, to illustrate repentance, he would do a back flip.

In the movie *Elmer Gantry*, many of Gantry's antics on the platform were copied from Billy Sunday. Sunday was roundly criticized, yet he was by far the most successful evangelist of his day. He was Dwight L. Moody and Billy Graham all wrapped up in one!

Interestingly, Billy Graham's father, Frank Graham, became a Christian in Billy Sunday's 1923 campaign in Charlotte, North Carolina. Mordecai Ham gets credit for Billy's conversion, but I think Billy Graham's daddy, Frank, might have had something to do with Billy Graham's conversion as well, and so Billy Sunday deserves some credit.

When I was a student in Washington D.C., our bishop was a very well-known and quite liberal bishop named John Wesley Lord. With a name like that, did he have any choice but to become a Methodist bishop? I was an impressionable seminarian in those days. These were the days of the Civil Rights marches and the peace protests, and our bishop was in the forefront of many of these events.

And yet one of the things that made the greatest impact on me as a young seminarian was to hear that very liberal, well-educated, intelligent and polished bishop say on one occasion that he had been converted in a Billy Sunday crusade.

It is estimated that over one million persons came to Christ during Billy Sunday's ministry. One million! And that was before radio and television. During the final part of his ministry, commercial radio had just begun, but television did not exist. They didn't even have PA systems for most of that time.

Whole cities would turn out for Sunday. His workers wouldn't simply go in and put up a tent, they would build a wooden cathedral that would hold 10,000 people for a Billy Sunday crusade. He was a fabulous organizer and promoter.

One reason Sunday was a great communicator was that he was conscious of colorful language. Take the familiar phrase, "Sitting in church doesn't make you a Christian any more than sitting in a garage makes you an automobile." Billy Sunday said that as soon as automobiles came out.

I'm not suggesting you do a back flip in the pulpit next Sunday, but if you want to move people, there has to be a certain element of drama.

Winston Churchill was an extraordinary actor. So were Fidel Castro, General Charles de Gaulle, Franklin Roosevelt and John Kennedy. Be dramatic. You must be guided by the laws of good taste and acceptability in your church. However, most of us will not go too far in that direction. Most of us would be rather too dull than dramatic. Who's willing to be a fool for Christ?

Remember that people respond to differing stimuli. Neuro-linguistic Programming (NLP) tells us that people have three primary modes of sensory perception—visual, auditory, and kinesthetic (kinesthetics are high touch/high feeling individuals).

I'm a high visual person. You can always tell a person who's primarily visual in their communication mode because when we're thinking we look up and to the side. When I'm trying to remember something, I look up to the left. When I'm trying to create something, I look up to the right. Theoretically, you ought to be able to tell when I'm lying because when you ask me about something that happened in the past and I look up and to the right, I'm creating, not remembering. That's called lying. I understand that's why our Arab friends wear sunglasses in negotiations, because they read eyes and they don't want anybody reading their eyes when they're negotiating.

Auditory people look to the side—toward their ears. Talk to a musician (except, perhaps, for pianists) and notice how often they look to the side when they're trying to remember or create something.

Kinesthetics look down and to the side. I saw Roger Williams, the pianist, on Robert Schuller's program one time. Schuller was recovering from falling and hitting his head. Roger Williams was asking for funds for Schuller's ministry while Schuller was incapacitated. I couldn't help thinking in a cynical way he was "shilling for Schuller." Actually, he did a great job. He was very sincere. I noticed that while he talked, he'd look to the side and down while he was thinking, then he'd look up to the camera. He's a high kinesthetic and that probably makes him a great pianist.

All of us are a combination of all three modes. For example, I've always wondered if the expression "downright mean" was derived from the fact that when most people are filled with strongly negative emotions, they will look down and to the right. Just wondering.

Apply your knowledge of these three modes to the preaching situation. You have folks in there who are high visuals, others who are auditory, some who are kinesthetics. Most worship services are designed for auditories. Right? So we have to build some things into the worship to help the visuals and the kinesthetics.

I listen to audio presentations when I'm on my treadmill for educational purposes. But I really don't get much out of listening to those presentations. Most of it's lost. I have to see something for it to stay with me because I'm a visual person. The worship service primarily caters to auditories. Our churches may have stain-glass windows or we may wear colorful stoles. And, of course, there are flowers on the altar, but all these are static. There's very little real visual stimulation. Thank God, we have the Lord's Supper for the kinesthetics. I have this theory that when a high kinesthetic comes to church, if somebody will just give him or her a hug, that will be the high point of the worship experience for that person.

We need to be conscious that we might not be ministering to all of our people by just standing in front of them and declaring the Word. We need to do things that are visual. We need to move around. We need to give them something that they can actually pass around and feel. It would be effective communication. The need for visual and kinesthetic stimulation in worship brings me to the next suggestion.

Use objects. Now, you probably already use objects in your children's sermon. Perhaps you've had the experience of having people come out after the service and say, "Hey, the children's sermon was the best part of the service this morning." The reason it was the best part of the service was that you used an object and you made a very simple point with that object. It was probably the only part of the service they understood. I'm exaggerating, of course. But why not use the same approach in communicating to adults?

I was flipping around the television channels years ago, and I caught Charles Stanley on television. Halfway through the service, Stanley took his handkerchief out of his pocket and waved it in the air and said, "Sometimes I feel like taking my handkerchief and using it as a white flag and just waving to God and saying, 'I surrender, I surrender.'" Later in that same service, he took his ball point pen out of his shirt pocket. He held that pen up and he said, "Somebody gave me this pen years ago and I really value it for that reason, it's a fine writing instrument. But one of these days, this pen is going to quit writing and when it does, do you know what I'm going to do? I'm going to put it in my desk drawer and I'll probably never see it again, because what good is a ball point pen that doesn't write." Then he put the pen down and he looked into the television camera, right at me and he said, "What good is a Christian who's no longer bearing fruit?" Did he get his point across? I think most people understood what he was saying.

I was in a service where the pastor was speaking on the yoke of Christ, and he had an actual yoke sitting behind the altar. In another service, a pastor was using the analogy of two boat oars to describe the relationship of faith and works, and he brought out a boat oar and he started to row while he talked. Let me hasten to say, these were not tiny backwoods churches, but rather large, sophisticated churches.

In another service in a relatively large church, I saw a lay leader take a balloon out of his pocket. He blew it up right there in the pulpit! "Sometimes I'm like this balloon," he said, "filled with the spirit of the living God. Other times," he said as he let the balloon go and we sat and watched with formal, pious expressions on our faces while that balloon whipped up into the air and then torpedoed suddenly downward and flopped flat on the floor, "Other times, I'm flatter than this balloon."

Corny? Maybe, but everybody in the room was paying attention—from age 3 to 93. It was sincere. It was simple. It worked.

Calvin Miller, in *Preaching: The Art of Narrative Exposition*, notes that for a sermon on "Treasures in Earthen Vessels," he took into the pulpit an old clay pot filled with the treasures of his life (wedding band, driver's license, ordination papers, etc.). Each of these artifacts had an accompanying story as he drew them from the pot.

The prophet Ezekiel was a master of dramatic actions. He constructed a model of a city under siege. He lay on his side for days. He cut his hair and beard with a razor and proceeded to burn some of it, throw some of it into the air and cut little parts of it into smaller pieces to symbolize the destruction of Jerusalem. Then he dug a tunnel under the city wall and dragged his possessions through it as a symbol of the coming Dispersion, while the people looked on in astonishment.

Jeremiah broke clay pots as a symbol of the coming judgment on Jerusalem and wore an ox yoke to convey the message that his nation would submit to Babylon.

We know that Isaiah presented himself stripped to a loin cloth, like a war prisoner or slave—representing the fact that Israel would be taken prisoner by Assyria. Object lessons, every one.

Jesus riding into Jerusalem on a donkey was an object lesson! We have plenty of precedents. Maybe Jesus was holding in his hands a lily of the field or a mustard seed as he told the relevant parables. We know he used bread and a cup on one occasion. Object lessons can be effective. Don't just save them for the children's sermons.

Of course, discretion is called for in using dramatic devices. In the January 1999 issue of *Esquire* magazine it was reported, "In an attempt to show his congregation that sin was like Russian roulette, Melvyn Nurse, a Florida minister, fatally injured himself when he pointed a pistol loaded with blanks at his head and fired, shooting a blank casing through his temple."

I will say this in his defense: this is one sermon his congregation will probably never forget. Some are probably still in therapy.

Make wise use of pauses. John Wayne once said that he believed his talent actually lay in the distinctive way he used a pause in the middle of each sentence. Use of the pause is particularly critical to the use of humor. We will discuss it further in that section.

Be conscious of your speaking voice. An actor, after listening to the Calvinist preacher George Whitefield, observed that this gripping evangelist could convert people simply by the way he said, "Mesopotamia." It was also said of Whitefield that he could address 10,000 people without a PA system. I don't have a voice that is that strong nor that dramatic. But that doesn't mean I can't work on my voice. And so can you.

It is said of Fred Craddock that because he had a weak, thin voice as a young preacher, he would go out to a nearby pasture regularly and preach to the cows. He thought if he could get Holsteins to raise their heads, he would be heard in churches. Hearing about Craddock's practice, Will Willimon told his students at Duke that, considering the congregations they would be addressing, he would strongly recommend this method of voice training.

Think about your voice for a moment. No one has a voice like yours. Your voice print is as distinctive as your fingerprint. Someday you'll walk up to your front door and speak to it and your door will automatically open. It will recognize your voice and a master impersonator won't be able to fool it. To a certain extent, you are your voice. If you are under stress, it will show in your voice. There is a machine that can measure this. It works as well as a lie detector.

Your voice shows your involvement in your subject. Have you ever noticed that people with bland personalities have bland voices? It's true! You are your voice. However you can train your speaking voice. Actors do. TV personalities do. Are they more committed to their craft than the local pastor? I don't mean that all of us need to sound like the deep-voiced guys who do motion picture previews, but there are some little things we can do.

Listen to yourself from time to time on a digital voice recorder. Whenever I go out to lead a seminar or workshop or speak at a church, I carry a voice recorder along. When I get back home, I'll put on my headset and listen to my voice . . . then cry.

It's humbling. I have this thin, rather high pitched voice, and you don't know how hard I have worked to make it acceptable for listening.

John Malloy, the well-known advisor on success in the business world, reports that 95% of American males can boost their voice power by lowering their speech tones. He says that the same percentage of women can boost their power, too, by not only lowering their voice but by slowing their speech as well. He claims that too many women tend to speak too quickly, thus losing their effectiveness.

A simple thing like volume may be critical. Invest in an excellent sound system if you have vocal shortcomings. Even in the smallest of churches, find a reason to make that investment. The amplified voice always sounds more dramatic. After all, no sound is more dramatic than a whisper and a good sound system will allow you to bring your voice down to a whisper when that is appropriate. Of course, many pastors have the opposite problem. They get too loud. Excessive volume can detract. Remember, it's lightning that kills people, not thunder. Lighten up if you have a tendency to be bombastic.

Of course, if reading from a manuscript, you will have to work harder at being dramatic than from an outline or extemporaneously. It can be done, but not without work.

One final note about the voice: watch your accent. I'm the last person in the world to say anything about an accent. If you have heard me speak, you know that I have a pronounced East Tennessee accent. When I first moved from the hills of east Tennessee to Washington D.C. to attend seminary, Gomer Pyle was one of the most popular programs on TV. People would say to me, "Why, you sound just like Gomer Pyle."

My wife is constantly on me to watch my accent. "People with southern Appalachian accents are looked upon as being slow-witted," she says. She's from South Carolina, big deal. But she's right, and believe it or not, I have improved.

It helped me to learn that in New Testament times, the Jewish Synagogue service ended with the very familiar blessing, "The Lord bless you and keep you. The Lord make his face to shine upon you and be gracious unto you. The Lord lift up his countenance upon you and give you peace."

That blessing was to be pronounced by a priest, if a priest was present, but there was a regulation: it must not be pronounced by a Galilean or by a person whose fingers were stained and on whose hand the stain could be seen when raised in the act of blessings.

Why the prohibition against Galileans? It is because they spoke with a characteristic burr. At the trial of Jesus, you remember, Peter in the courtyard of the high priest was recognized as a Galilean because his accent gave him away. It was a rural accent—an Appalachian-type accent, if you will. The point of the Jewish regulation was that nothing—whether it be the Galilean accent or the stain on the hand—nothing should distract the attention of the worshipper.

Sometimes an accent can be used to great effect. I think of all of those Presbyterian preachers from Scotland who prosper in this country. Part of it has to do with the accent and part of it is the authenticity of their message, but accents can be important. Be sure that yours contributes, rather than detracts.

Check the expression on your face. Several years ago, Doctor Albert Mehrabian, a UCLA communication researcher startled the communications field with a study on nonverbal communication. According to Mehrabian, there are three elements to oral acts of communication, and each has an impact on what audiences receive and what they believe. Here is how they stack up. What you say accounts for 7% of what is believed. The way you say it accounts for 38%. And what the audiences sees while you are saying it accounts for a whopping 55% of what the audience believes!

If your voice says one thing and your face says another, they are going to believe your face. Be conscious of how you look. A pleasant expression on your face generally helps. Have you ever seen somebody talking about the grace of God—along with the love and acceptance which comes from God—and do it with a scowl on their face? The wrong thing is probably being communicated. "What you are speaks so loudly that I can't hear what you say."

You bring more into the pulpit than just your words. From the expression on your face and your body language I can sense at least five things. I can sense when you are in a bad mood. I can sense whether you like me. I can sense when you are unprepared. I can sense your commitment to your subject. I can sense whether you enjoy preaching. Are these important considerations? They each can make or break a sermon.

I love the story of the self-announced expert whose eyes fell on an interesting face, a little pale, slightly drawn with a certain glassiness in the eyes. "Here," he added, "is a preacher—a Methodist preacher."

A moment's hush, and then the answer, softly spoken: "You got me wrong, brother, I'm no preacher; I just have stomach ulcers."

Watch your gestures. Now, I realize that gestures come more naturally to some people than to others. An old Jewish peddler was ambling down a street in Tel Aviv carrying two large watermelons when a tourist stopped him and asked, "Where is Bin Yehuda Street?"

The peddler answered, "Please hold these two watermelons."

The tourist managed to collect those two watermelons in his arms, whereupon the peddler made an expansive gesture and exclaimed, "How should I know?"

Again, I think it may be better to err on the side of being too demonstrative than standing like a wooden soldier. Beginning speakers ask, "What should I do with my hands?" The answer is, "Forget them. Do what comes naturally."

Hamlet approaches his band of players before a rehearsal to offer some theatrical advice. Waving his hand, he tells them, "Nor do not saw the air too much with your hand, thus," adding, "Suit the action to the word, the word to the action." [35]

I know that if I do not consciously avoid it, out of nervous energy, I have a tendency to saw the air while I talk. Such sawing adds energy to my speaking. It is also the sign of an amateur. Every gesture should be appropriate to what you are trying to say. Stand in front of a full-length mirror with a large book in each hand. When you raise your hands, these are real gestures—others are nervous gestures. [36] For a long time, I requested a hand-held mike so that at least one of my hands would be occupied and, therefore, still as I spoke.

Voltaire once tied the hands of a would-be actress who was in the habit of overdoing her gestures. They came across as fake and so he tied her hands with thread and gave her a speech to recite. Finally, in a crescendo of passion, this actress raised her hands and broke the threads. She was embarrassed. Voltaire reassured her. He told her that what he had hoped she would do was use gestures when her enthusiasm became so great she couldn't help it. So, she had done the right thing. She had broken the threads when she could no longer help but use her hands.

If you forget your hands and do what comes naturally, you will be on solid ground. Don't be afraid to use gestures. Be conscious of those gestures, however, particularly the use of the fist or the pointed finger. Avoid weak, meaningless gestures like fiddling with your glasses, reaching into your pocket and unconsciously jiggling change, repeatedly pushing back your hair, buttoning and unbuttoning a coat, or using any single gesture over and over and over again.

Ask questions. How does the book of Jonah end? It ends with a question. You know the story. Jonah runs away from God, is swallowed by a fish, the fish spits him up, Jonah decides he'd better do what God wants; finally, he preaches to Nineveh and the whole city repents. It was the greatest revival in history—everybody repents, from the king on down. Jonah should be elated, but he is miserable. Why? Because he has been telling the Ninevites that they're going to be destroyed, and God changes his mind. Jonah feels foolish and becomes so angry he sits on a hillside and says, "I'm going to sit here until I die or until God destroys Nineveh."

Jonah's sitting there, the sun's beating down, it gets hotter and hotter. Jonah's wondering, why did I ever say that? But he's stubborn. Finally, God sends a gourd plant to shade Jonah. The plant grows up during the night and provides him some shade the next day. He thinks, "Whew, I regret making that decision, but I'm glad this plant's here to shade me." That night, God sends a worm to eat up the gourd plant in one night. Jonah looks around and there's no longer any shade. He's still going to sit there until he dies, but that gourd plant is gone and he is angrier than ever. He thinks God is toying with him. He's about to pop a blood vessel. And God comes to him and asks him a question. "Jonah, you're so concerned about that plant that grew up in the night and then died in the night. Should I not be concerned about this great city of Nineveh where there are 145 thousand people who know not their right hand from their left and also much cattle?" That's the way it ends. It just leaves us hanging with a question. We go out and get the car and drive home, and we're still thinking about that question.

Who shot J.R.? Think of the impact that question made all over our country. Billy Graham answered that question in a sermon. Billy Graham said, "I'll tell you who shot J.R. A sinner shot J.R." Questions can be excellent rhetorical devices. There is a difference between saying, "Everybody gets angry from time to time" than saying, "Have there been times in your life when you have been so upset that you could not contain yourself?" You see, the former drives people away. The latter draws them in by asking questions.

These can be rhetorical questions, of course. I'll never forget preaching my first sermon as a student pastor to a small rural Maryland congregation and beginning that message with a hot question of the day, "Is God dead? Is God dead?" And then I waited and I waited. Looking back, I realize my congregation wasn't sure after that message whether God was dead or not. But it was dramatic.

The rhetorical question must be used well, or not at all. Personally, I prefer real questions. "Simon Peter had a brother, his name was . . ." Let the congregation tell you his name. "They were of what profession?" Let them answer. "That's right. They were fisherman, but Christ told them they would be what?" And somebody will speak up and say "Fishers of men." Even in a large church, that kind of simple dialogue can be refreshing. Of course, you have to be careful.

I love the late Sam Ervin's story about the preacher who one night after the sermon called on the members of the congregation to testify about what the good Lord had done for them. No one volunteered. He asked again. Still nobody spoke, whereupon he called upon poor Uncle Henry who was infirm and stooped with arthritis. "Uncle Henry tell us what the Lord has done for you?" the preacher said.

The old man got up slowly and laboriously. He straightened himself up and finally said, "Well, he's mighty nigh near killed me." It helps if you know the answer before you ask.

Use repetition. In an oral event, repetition is essential. Repetition both adds drama and aids memory. When President Bill Clinton spoke at the fiftieth anniversary of D-Day, he made masterful use of repetition: "They were the fathers we never knew, the uncles we never met, the friends who never returned, the heroes we can never repay." It's hard to improve on that.

A blushing young woman handed a telegraph clerk a telegraph containing only a name, address and one word, "Yes!"

Wishing to be helpful, the clerk said, "You know, you can send 9 more words for the same price."

"I know, I can," replied the young woman. "But don't you think I'd look too eager if I said it 10 times?"

I'm not certain she could have said it too many times, are you? I'm not certain I ever heard a preacher use too much repetition. Usually, too little is used. In an oral presentation, if you don't repeat something time and time again there'll be people who'll miss what it is you really wanted to say.

A justice to the Supreme Court once told Charles Finney that many pastors err at just this point. "When a lawyer has a jury in front of him—respectable men, intelligent men—but that lawyer knows if he doesn't repeat his major positions about as many times as there are persons on the jury, he risks losing his case." If there are twelve people on a jury, a good lawyer will repeat his main contention twelve times.

I first ran across Finney's statement during the William Kennedy Smith trial some time back. Trial attorney Roy Black, the defense lawyer, referred to his main premise more than one hundred times in the course of that trial. That's repetition.

Would you happen to remember this little phrase? "If it doesn't fit, you must acquit." Is repetition powerful in oral communication? Are you kidding me?

If there is a point that you believe is vital to make, you need to say it time and time again. Now, that could get monotonous if you just repeated the same thing over and over. There are some devices by which you can use repetition creatively.

The first is the contrast. For example, "Ask not what your country can do for you, rather ask what you can do for your country." John F. Kennedy said that 35 or 40 years ago, but it's still a beautiful part of our national consciousness.

Let's go from the sublime to the ridiculous. "If guns are outlawed, only outlaws will have guns." You've heard that some time or another. "When the going gets tough, the tough get going." Or its feminine counterpart: "When the going gets tough, the tough go shopping." That's a contrast or paired element.

The Bible is filled with contrasts—light and dark, good and evil, clean and unclean. "You have heard it said . . . but I say to you," Jesus used the contrast or paired element one hundred and forty two times. The man knew how to communicate. The contrast or paired element is very pleasing to the ear. And it makes your words memorable.

The second device is the triad. As you might guess the triad is a list of three: "Man is born, man lives, man dies." Lincoln used the triad masterfully in the Gettysburg Address: "government of the people, by the people, for the people." You and I can use it, too: "Jesus is our Savior. Jesus is our Redeemer. Jesus is our Lord."

The third is the continuum. The continuum is one of the most effective and yet least-used devices that preachers employ. A continuum is repeating the same phrase or idea in a rising crescendo five or more times.

Our nation will never forget Martin Luther King, standing before the Washington monument, declaring, "I have a dream!" Time and time again, he spelled out what that dream was. "I have a dream!" "I have a dream!" I don't know why this device seems to be the exclusive domain of Black preachers. Perhaps it's because they understand the oral nature of preaching.

Tony Campolo used this device so beautifully as he portrayed his African-American pastor in Philadelphia on Good Friday saying, "It's Friday and my Jesus is hanging dead on a tree. But it's Friday, and Sunday's coming.

"It's Friday, and Mary's crying her eyes out and the disciples are scattered like sheep without a shepherd. But it's Friday, and Sunday's coming."

And he keeps working that device. "It's Friday, but Sunday's coming. It's Friday, but Sunday's coming. It's Friday, but Sunday's coming" until he reaches the climax of that great message. And he shouts out, "It's Friday!" and the whole congregation stands up and with one accord shouts back, "But Sunday's coming!"

Friend, that's preaching. Sometime you ought to try writing a sermon with a continuum in it, just to see if you can do it, just for the fun of it, the exhilaration. And you don't have to use complete sentences to make use of a continuum.

I'll never forget the first time I heard the old radio preacher J. Vernon McGhee use the familiar refrain about money that goes something like this:

Money can buy a house, but it can't buy a home;

Money can buy a diamond, but it can't buy love;

Money can buy the services of a doctor, but it can't buy health;

Money can buy a bed, but it can't buy sleep;

Money can buy a book, but it can't buy knowledge;

Money can buy a clock, but it can't buy time;

Money can buy a position, but it can't buy respect;

Money can buy a church pew, but it can't buy salvation.

That captures the ear and is memorable. Nobody used contrasts in a continuum better than the writer of Ecclesiastes:

There is a time for everything, and a season for every activity under the heavens:

a time to be born and a time to die, a time to plant and a time to uproot,

a time to kill and a time to heal, a time to tear down and a time to build,

a time to weep and a time to laugh, a time to mourn and a time to dance,

a time to scatter stones and a time to gather them,

a time to embrace and a time to refrain from embracing, a time to search and a time to give up,

a time to keep and a time to throw away, a time to be silent and a time to speak,

a time to love and a time to hate, a time for war and a time for peace. (3:1-8)

The continuum is a powerful, powerful tool as you can see. It is dramatic. It builds involvement. It allows for creative repetition.

When you are writing, such devices are not necessary. But in an oral presentation, repetition is essential. Of course, you don't have to limit yourself to either three or five items in your list. St. Paul sometimes use four items, and he was pretty effective: "Love bears all things, believes all things, hopes all things, endures all things." (I Corinthians 13:7, RSV).

Repetition is not only helpful within the body of your messages but also repetition is a wonderful device as an ongoing tool through all of your ministry. Cato the Elder has been famous through the centuries because for years he ended every one of his remarks in the Roman Senate with these words: "Carthage must be destroyed!"

W. A. Criswell once said that he mentioned tithing in every sermon he ever preached. I don't know how you do that. But Criswell did, and it worked. Repetition sells.

Use eye contact. I have had pastors tell me that they were trained to preach to a spot on the back wall rather than look people in the eye as they preached. How sad. John Wesley said, "Look your audience decently in the face, one after another, as we do in familiar conversation." You won't get better advice than that. You should look individual people in various parts of the sanctuary directly in the eye for from 4 to 6 seconds. Any less than that and you will not be connecting. Any more than that—particularly if it's a member of the opposite sex—and you may get yourself into trouble. Garrison Keillor of *Prairie Home Companion* fame once quipped, "A preacher is a person who engages in far more eye contact than people want." It's terrifying for some pastors, but it is essential to effective communication.

There is an amusing anecdote about President Ulysses S. Grant. When General Grant became President, he learned to combat his embarrassment while conversing with diplomats; he looked at the end of their noses. One observer commented that noses, curiously enough, are easier to dominate than eyes. The secret? The person at whose nose we gaze assumes that we are looking him squarely in the eye. For even at short range, he can't tell the difference. If, then, you dislike to look at eyes, why not try noses instead? [37] Whatever works.

Remember, you are not building a case when you are in the pulpit as much as you are seeking to build a relationship with everyone in the room. Eye contact therefore is essential. Start with someone who is supportive—if no one is supportive, pack it up.

Make extensive use of dialogue. Dialogue keeps your sermon active and moving. Rather than saying about a farm couple that John turned to Mary and suggested that they plough the field that day, help us to hear the conversation. John turns to Mary and with a sense of urgency says, "Honey, I think it's time to plough the field." You see, that's more active than simply using indirect discourse. Just by adding direct quotes, you add movement to your sermon, you make it more real. So be conscious of doing that every opportunity you have.

Abraham Lincoln was one of our country's great story-tellers. "They say I tell a great many stories," he once said, "and I reckon I do. But I have learned from long experience that plain people are more easily influenced through the medium of a broad and humorous illustration than in any other way." [38]

In her book, *Corporate Legends and Lore*, Peg Neuhauser tells one of Lincoln's favorites. It seems that there was this colonel who proposed to his men that he would do all the swearing for the regiment. They agreed, and for months everyone controlled their profanity and let the colonel do all the swearing for the group. The driver of the mule team, John Todd, had a difficult time controlling his temper as he maneuvered his mule team over rough roads. Finally one day, the mud holes being particularly bad, John couldn't stand it anymore, and he burst forth into a volley of profanity. The colonel heard about his offense and confronted John saying, "Didn't you promise to let me do all the swearing for the regiment?"

According to Lincoln, John replied, "Yes, I did, Colonel, but the fact was the swearing had to be done then or not at all, and you weren't there to do it."

Note how Lincoln switched to specific quotes. He not only tells us about the conversation; he lets us listen in on the action. [39] This makes the interaction livelier.

Be mindful of movement. We live in a movement oriented society, don't we? If we have to wait 24 seconds on an elevator, we get nervous. We live in a day of the one-minute manager and the one-minute parent and the one-minute lover. I understand there's a book called *The 59 Second Employee: How to Stay One Step Ahead of the One-Minute Manager.* [40]

We are a very movement conscious society. Any place you can add movement, either in the structure of your sermon or in the way you present it, do it. I personally like pastors who move around as they preach, as long as it is meaningful movement. As in the use of gestures, your enemy is excessive nervous energy if it causes you to pace back and forth or do a little dance as you preach. (I've been guilty of both.)

On the positive side, there's nothing more boring than something that never moves. As someone has said, "Podiums are poison; lecterns are lethal." Add movement wherever you can.

More Tips for Elevating Your Preaching

Know your people. David A. McLennan uses the word *curé* to describe this function of the pastor/preacher. This is what the parish priest is called in French-speaking countries. It's a good word. You are there to act as a *curé* to your people. You are to know them and love them.

Some years back Edgar Jackson did a survey in which he discovered that in the average congregation, 20% will be struggling with an acute sense of loss. Thirty-three percent will have serious marriage problems, including spousal abuse. Fifty percent have problems of adjustment in work, school, community or home. Five percent are battling depression—sometime serious depression, which may manifest itself in character disorders like infidelity, gambling, alcoholism, etc. Twenty percent are dealing with serious guilt or fear.
41

It's interesting that 45% to 55% of Americans who convert or return to their former church say they did it because they needed help with their family life. That says to me that pastors should use the pulpit more to address family issues. The question is not "How do I preach a superior sermon today?" The question is, "What are my people's needs and how can I go about meeting those needs?"

An author of 20 best sellers was asked her secret. She answered, "I just write books that help people." Joseph Parker, a great preacher of yesteryear, once said to a group of aspiring young ministers, "Preach to the suffering and you will never lack a congregation. There is a broken heart in every pew."

Charles E. Jefferson says we should always remember the line from the story of the feeding of the 5000, "There is a lad here."

Remember the children as you preach. There may be a lad or a lass there who has something to offer to Christ. How can I meet that young person's need? Or how can I meet the needs of moms and dads, and how can I meet the needs of older people? Preaching that is not centered in applying the gospel to human need is a performance, not a sermon.

Remember, you are the neediest one of all. Try to say "we" from the pulpit, not "you." Except in the most authoritarian churches, there will be a psychological rejection of pastors who are always talking about "you sinners;" say "we sinners." Remember the story of the pastor conducting services at the state mental institution who had one of the inmates say, "Oh brother Jones, we do look forward to your visits. Somehow you seem just like one of us." Well, that's one of the highest compliments you can be paid. Identify with your people, ask them questions about their life and about their spiritual needs.

Rick Warren says, "Notice the total emphasis on felt needs and hurts. When you are in pain, either physically or emotionally, you aren't interested in the meaning of Greek and Hebrew words. You just want to get well. Jesus always ministered to people's needs and hurts. When a leper came to Jesus, Jesus didn't launch into a long discourse on the cleansing laws of Leviticus. He just healed the man! When he encountered the sick, the demon-possessed, or the disturbed, he dealt with them at their point of pain. He didn't say, 'I'm sorry, that doesn't fit my preaching schedule. Today we're continuing our series through the book of Deuteronomy.'" [42]

One reason sermon preparation is so difficult for many pastors is because they ask the wrong question. Instead of asking, "What shall I preach on this Sunday?" they should be asking, "To whom will I be preaching?" Simply thinking through the needs of the congregation will help determine God's will for the message.

Here's a quote from an article in the *Houston Chronicle*, August 29, 1992: "Pollster George H. Gallup, Jr. says 70 percent of Americans believe most churches and synagogues are not effective in helping people find meaning in life." He said the ongoing vitality of American religious congregations depends, in large measure, on their effectiveness in responding to six spiritual needs of Americans as identified in his surveys: 1. To believe life is meaningful and has a purpose. 2. To have a sense of community and deeper relationships. 3. To be appreciated and respected. 4. To be listened to—and heard. 5. To feel that one is growing in the faith. 6. To have practical help in developing a mature faith. [43]

Discover their needs and do some research. I know your time is limited. Still, if you're preaching a sermon on depression, it would not hurt to do some extra research on depression. Then you may be able to say something fresh to your people on this important subject—for example, the role of repressed anger in depression. People enjoy getting new insights into both the scriptures and themselves. If you speak on a rather complicated subject off the top of your head, you cheat yourself out of the opportunity to acquire a new sense of authority with your people and you cheat them out of the opportunity to receive some concrete help. Know your people and your subject.

Exploit your personality. In his lectures on preaching, Phillips Brooks gave the most profound definition of preaching that we have. "Preaching is the communication of truth by man to men. It has 2 essential elements, truth and personality. Neither of those can [it spare] and still be preaching."

Truth and personality, both are essential to an effective message. The most effective preacher is the one who can most easily be himself or herself in the pulpit. Be yourself. Be natural. Do not be defeated if you are not naturally gifted.

Pastors often make one of two mistakes. There are some pastors who spend their whole ministry imitating somebody else. We had a pastor who came to our town a few years back who, if you closed your eyes and listened to him preach, you would swear Billy Graham was in the pulpit. I mean, every nuance--it was clear that he had studied Graham and listened to him enough so that he just copied him completely.

Now that's fine. A lot of Southern Baptist pastors sound like Billy Graham. Except that this guy was from New Jersey and he was of Italian-American heritage. How does an Italian-American from New Jersey end up sounding like Billy Graham from North Carolina? You see, it was just incredible. He was very popular for about a year, but I noticed after a year his popularity started to wane, and he was gone after about two years. This wasn't a small church; it was a rather large church. But folks don't go to their local church to hear Billy Graham, unless Billy Graham is preaching. They come to hear their pastor.

The greatest thing you have going for you is you. It's alright if you subconsciously pattern yourself after someone who has had a major influence on you. But there are some pastors who never go beyond that.

The other thing I see is that some pastors hide their personality under a bushel. Some pastors never relax and enjoy being themselves in the pulpit. And that's sad. I'll visit with a pastor friend of mine and we'll be cutting up in the study beforehand. Then I'll go and sit down in the congregation and he will go up in the pulpit and sometimes it's amazing the transformation that takes place between the study and the pulpit. This guy I've been having such a terrific time with, laughing and cutting up in the study, becomes so somber and he talks with this great stained-glass voice. I'll be sitting out there in the pew thinking, where did he go? That guy that I was having such a great time with. Where is he? Who is this up there in the pulpit?

The "magic bullet" of personal communications, says communication guru Roger Ailes, is the quality of being likeable. Think about that for a moment and ponder the implications for pastors.

United Press International released the results of a poll years ago concerning TV and film stardom. The result of that poll was that the main element in stardom is likeability. The same thing is true in politics. The most important factor in getting elected is likeability. In a Gallup poll taken during each presidential election since 1960, voters have been asked to rate the candidates based upon three criteria: their stand on the issues, their party affiliation, and their likeability. The candidate who scored highest in the likeability category has won every election. [44]

"Likeability," says Roger Ailes, "is difficult to define or to teach, but the basic positives that reside in the likeable person are (1) optimism, (2) concern about the welfare of other people, (3) ability to see the opportunity in every difficulty, (4) ability to handle stress, (5) ability to laugh easily, especially at himself, and (6) ability to perform at his best in crises and at his humblest in prosperity." [45] That wouldn't be a bad set of characteristics for the leader of a local congregation.

It's said that actress Mary Martin, before going on the stage, would close her eyes, take a deep breath, and say 100 times to herself, "I love my audience." Next she would repeat the process, but this time tell herself, "My audience loves me." That would be a worthy practice for pastors.

The pastor of a church sets the tone and atmosphere of the congregation. If you are a pastor, someone has said, and you want to know the warmth of your church, put a thermometer in your own mouth. I've visited some churches where the pastor's lack of love is the main reason the church isn't growing. Some pastors, by their cold demeanor and lack of personal warmth, virtually guarantee that visitors won't come back. Some of us are simply shy. It is not in our nature to reach out to others. For us, taking up the cross of Christ may be as simple as overcoming our introversion and communicating to people that we really do care for them.

Preaching is truth through personality. When the word is effective it becomes flesh, and friend, you're the flesh on Sunday morning. And you'll be most effective when you just relax.

You'll say, "Well, King, I don't have a very good personality." Neither do I. Seriously. I'm an introvert's introvert. That doesn't mean I don't love to laugh. That doesn't mean I don't love to tell a good story. It means that I have to get in touch with that inner "social me" that I keep buried most of the time. Before I go into the pulpit, I pray that God will be with me and then I say to myself, "Whatever happens today, I'm going to have a good time in the pulpit." And I do. I'm well prepared. I am confident in my material, and I seek to transfer that over into my presentation.

It's work for me. I envy my present pastor, Mark Flynn, who has an irrepressible personality and could talk for hours on any subject. He's a remarkably effective communicator. But that's not me. I will just have to work harder and add more value to my presentations by the fact that I have prepared so well. The only way you can be effective is to be genuinely yourself. Credibility is the most important thing in today's world and that flows from authenticity. Be yourself.

In his book *Streams of Living Water*, Richard Foster tells of Billy Graham preaching at Cambridge in 1955. For three nights he tried to make his preaching academic and enlightened, but with no effect. Graham finally realized that presenting the intellectual side of faith was not his gift and began preaching the simple message of Jesus rescuing us from our sin. Foster writes, "The results were astonishing: hundreds of sophisticated students responded to this clear presentation of the Gospel..." [46]

The elder President George H. W. Bush was quoted as saying during a presidential campaign, "You don't know how hard it's been for me to keep my charisma in check for the past 8 years." Bush is not naturally gifted in many ways but he's done all right in the world. You may not have a silver tongue but if you are authentic, you can still be a great preacher. You can get the job done that God has called you to do.

A study a while back showed that poor delivery may inhibit immediate attitudinal change. But it does not damage the credibility of the speaker. That is people give much higher marks to your sincerity than you might imagine. In this sense, the medium truly is the message, and when you stand in the pulpit, you are the medium. There are very few born preachers. Some of the best pulpiteers have overcome tremendous obstacles. Remember what we said before, preaching is the art of good conversation. Work at being an interesting person. But above all, be yourself. Be authentic. Be real. Let your personality shine through. Be yourself amplified.

Preach with purpose. James R. Peterson, former president of Pillsbury, says he begins preparing for every speaking occasion by asking, "What is my headline?" The headline is not the title of his presentation, but it's a short description of the presentation's main objective. Every sermon should have a main theme that directs the development of the sermon. Haddon Robinson calls this "the big idea." [47]

You should be able to state in a simple sentence what your purpose is for a particular message. It may be "I want to help my people experience the majesty of God." Can you see that stating that purpose beforehand will affect such things as your choice of language and imagery, as well as the kind of illustrations you choose? "I want to create a sense of closeness and fellowship within my church family." Can you see how such a purpose might affect even your posture and your body language as well as your content? Have a clear purpose as you prepare your message and as you mount the pulpit. Be as specific about your purpose as possible.

The best preachers are driven by an overall vision of their ministry. A vision is simply a picture of something that ought to happen. Nehemiah had a vision of rebuilding the city of Jerusalem. You may have a vision of rebuilding an inner city neighborhood or reaching Generation X. Visions come in all shapes and sizes. But vision is essential to leadership as well as to preaching. Without a vision, as someone has said, we are like an octopus on roller skates: we are all over the place and going nowhere.

Vision creates excitement. I have believed for a long time that the most essential ingredient in church growth is excitement. Surveys show that the majority of people who are new members in a church came because someone invited them. Your job is to cause so much excitement that your people will want to invite their friends. Excitement ought to pervade your ongoing program, but also what happens in the pulpit. People who visit growing churches come away saying one thing, "That church is so exciting." Well, which came first—the chicken or the egg? Is a church exciting because it is growing, or is it growing because it is exciting? The answer is, of course, both. A church will not grow without some measure of excitement and a growing church is an exciting place to be. We should not demean this fact.

Somehow, when I graduated from seminary I had the idea that success was a dirty word. A voice somewhere deep in my subconscious said to me, "If you are successful, you must be selling out."

As a young pastor, I sometimes led singing in revivals (yes, I know I am dating myself) for a very popular young evangelist. Secretly, I resented his silly jokes and his simple theology. "He's playing to the gallery," I said to myself. "How sad."

It was sad—sad that in my sanctimonious, pseudo-sophistication I did not realize that I was missing the point of preaching. Preaching is the task of connecting God with people. We are bridge builders. Call it playing to the gallery, if you please. It was the gallery for which Christ died.

Certainly, Jesus played to the gallery. Enormous crowds followed him wherever he went. Matthew 4:25 says, "Large crowds from Galilee, the Decapolis, Jerusalem, Judea and the region across the Jordan followed him." Matthew 7:28 says, "The crowds were amazed at his teaching." The multitudes had never heard anyone speak to them the way Jesus did. Jesus used humor. He told great stories. He used object lessons. He engaged their hearts, their minds and ultimately their commitment. Jesus was an exciting communicator. He is the standard by which we should evaluate our humble attempts to communicate the Gospel.

A letter was addressed to the General Electric Company from a little girl in the third grade who had chosen to investigate electricity for her class project. "I'm trying to get all the information I can," her letter said, "so please send me any booklets and papers you have. Also, would it be asking too much for you to send me a little sample of electricity?" Could you put a little sample of electricity in your preaching?

A certain husband wanted to cheer up his ailing wife. He went into the kitchen with the idea of baking some fresh bread. He gathered ingredients. On the counter he carefully assembled the flour, shortening, milk, yeast, etc. Somehow he misplaced the directions, however. So into the batter he added several packets of yeast—many times more than that called for by the recipe. After all, he reasoned, if a little yeast is good, a lot of yeast would be better. A little later his wife called downstairs, "Honey, have you put the bread in the oven?"

The distraught husband yelled from the kitchen, "In the oven? I can't keep it in the kitchen!"

What is the yeast you could add to your preaching to cause it to act like that? The key to church growth, then, is to get your folks so excited about their church that they invite others. Vision creates excitement. I like what Rick Warren says: "Where there is no vision, people move to another parish."

My wife and I were once members of a church that had a pastor who was the dullest preacher in all of Christendom. Now I haven't heard all the pastors in Christendom, but I doubt that this is an exaggeration. This fellow had refined tedium to an art-form. But every once in a while, he would catch a vision of what God could accomplish through our church, which was in a rapidly growing community. And when he got excited, we got excited. It was wonderful! Begin each message with a statement of purpose. What is it you want to happen with that message?

Make an outline of your message. Peter de Vries once said about writing, "Every novel should have a beginning, a muddle and an end." Well, that's also true of sermons. An outline is simply the skeleton of the sermon. The outline defines the contours of the sermon and helps the sermon move from one thought to another.

Grady Davis uses the analogy of a jigsaw puzzle. I think that's a good analogy, a jigsaw puzzle in which you hand a person first the blues for the sky, then the greens for the meadow, and then the blacks for the plowed earth at the bottom of the picture. As he states, "If I hand him the pieces one at a time in the right order, if he does not have to pick out the right one out of the handful of various shapes and sizes, the connection will be obvious, and he can put them together as we go along." The most important time you spend is that creative process of developing an outline. This outline can be propositional or it can be narrative, but you need to know beforehand where your message is headed.

Reuel Howe in his extensive study of preaching said that the one complaint of most lay people is that sermons are too complicated. The outline is where you attack that. I don't know why so many pastors resist making an outline. It is so important.

Have a strong introduction. Somewhere I saw a cartoon; a preacher is in the pulpit, someone is attaching battery cables to his ears. Underneath is the caption, "Sometimes our pastor needs a little help getting started." The first few moments in the pulpit are so, so important.

Some years ago, researchers polled a list of top speakers. One of the questions asked was, which part of your speech is the most fixed, written out, and all but memorized? The answer was the introduction. Great speakers and great preachers recognize the importance of a strong introduction. The introduction is where you hook the listener into the concern for the day.

George Buttrick advised that we should not reach the second paragraph of our sermon without convincing the person in the pew that what we are talking about is their concern. The question often arises where the strongest material in a sermon ought to be—at the beginning or at the end? Now, you may disagree, but studies show that it should generally be at the beginning.

Researcher Harold Sponberg prepared two phonograph records of the same material, but changed the order of presenting the material. To one group of students, he presented the speech in a traditional form. To the other group of students, he presented the speech in a revised form with the strongest point first and the other points following in order of their strength. Later, he examined both groups on the three points. What had they remembered? How had their minds been changed? After a lapse of time, he asked further questions that checked their memories.

He found that his students remembered better, remembered longer, and were more affected by the talk that presented the strong point first. So the rule, generally, put your strong point at the beginning. Whatever it is that you want people to really remember, you better say it up front. Now, there are exceptions to every rule. Some material begs to be at the conclusion. It may be that you're an artist with words and you can build toward a wonderful climax. Do it. However, few things will doom a sermon as much as a weak introduction. Even if you preach a narrative sermon that requires the strongest point at the end, you still must have a great introduction if you're going to have a great sermon.

One word of caution though. I know a pastor who has good intentions but he never follows through with his intentions. He starts off on Monday and writes a terrific introduction, then gets busy with well doing and ends up writing the rest of his message in a flurry on Saturday night. Result, his introduction is generally mind-boggling, which only serves to emphasize how sorry the rest of the message is. I have read one professor of Homiletics who says it's dangerous to have an introduction that's too good if the rest of the sermon is only mediocre.

There are many ways of getting your message off to a flying start. For example, the rhetorical question is a tried-and-true method. Or you may begin with a thought-provoking statement, an off-beat illustration, a striking quotation, or a current news item that is relevant. The introduction is a great place for humor.

The wonderful preacher of an earlier generation, Carlyle Marney, had a heart attack in the pulpit of his church, the Myers Park Baptist Church in Charlotte. Six months later, he returned to that pulpit. His first words were, "As I was saying . . ." He brought the house down.

Watch your language. I'm not worried about you using profanity from the pulpit, though I notice that some pastors are getting a little crude. That grates me the wrong way, but I am an old fuddy-duddy. If these pastors are connecting with their target audience, I'm not going to complain. We have a new generation saturated with crude language. Better to reach them in their vernacular than to scare them off by appearing to be totally out of touch. But we still need to watch our language.

Keep your language simple and concise. First test of a boring sermon–how long are the sentences–how long are the paragraphs? One analyst notes that television shows, even critically acclaimed series, are notoriously simplistic in their use of language. Script analyses of popular television shows such as *South Park*, *24*, *CSI*, *American Idol*, and *Friday Night Lights* all reveal a preponderance of monosyllabic words and short sentences.

Language simplification is apparent in cinema, as well. Film scripts from *Avatar*, *Planet of the Apes*, *Transformers*, *Lord of the Rings*, and *Star Wars* are written at a second- or third-grade readability level. The basic unit of communication for film is the image, with music and special effects playing significant, supplementary roles. Words serve only as minor support.[48]

Use the language of storytelling. What kind of language do we use when we tell a story? Once upon a time . . . one syllable words chiefly, simple language, concrete imagery. In classical preaching, the goal was to intellectually persuade people. Even your language was one of the proofs. You would quote certain authorities because that would add weight. Do you know that 99 percent of the folks in your congregation couldn't care less what Dietrich Bonhoeffer said about anything? Now you need to know what Dietrich Bonhoeffer said, and you need to tell Bonhoeffer's story. But if you think simply quoting Bonhoeffer adds credibility to a sermon, you are mistaken. You'd be better quoting Warren Buffet or Steven Hawkings.

There was a time when the pastor was the best-educated person in the community and you could impress people with a lofty vocabulary. Friend, that day is gone. You read the best writers today and they write in short, simple sentences. They use one syllable words wherever possible. And really, all the great words are one syllable words, aren't they? Faith, hope, love, fear, doubt, guilt, sin, etc. Almost every great word is a one syllable word. It's important to speak in a vocabulary that can be understood by everybody in the room.

I read a survey one time that showed that of the one hundred largest churches in this country, 75 are served by pastors who are not seminary graduates. Now that may say a lot of things to us. One thing I believe it says is that these pastors have not forgotten how to talk the language of the person in the pew. This is something that happens to a lot of us when we go to seminary. We come out speaking what can only be called "preacher-eze."

A Southern Baptist pastor came up to me after a workshop in Atlanta. He's a Southern Baptist moderate. He was very much in pain over the fundamentalist takeover of the Southern Baptist convention. He dealt with his pain with a joke: "King, I guess you heard about the time Jesus was going down the street and he ran into three men. The first man was blind and Jesus said, 'What can I do for you?' The man said, 'I'm blind,' and Jesus said, 'Receive your sight.' The man immediately could see. He came to the second man and asked, 'What can I do for you?' The man says, 'I'm lame.' Jesus said, 'Be healed.' The man jumped up and was totally healed. Jesus came to the third man and asked, 'What can I do for you?' The man said, 'I'm a Southern Baptist preacher,' and Jesus sat down and wept."

That was his way of dealing with his pain. But here's what he said to me, "King, I graduated from seminary about 20 years ago. When I got out of seminary, I discovered that I spoke an entirely different language and had a different set of values and a different operating style from any of my people. In 20 years, I have not been able to overcome that barrier." Can you relate to that? It's a deadly thing.

British writer C. S. Lewis once gave advice in a letter to a 12-year-old in Florida about writing. Here are a few things he said: "Always try to use the language so as to make quite clear what you mean and make sure your sentence couldn't mean anything else . . . Always prefer the plain, direct word to the long, vague one. Don't implement promises, but keep them . . . Never use abstract nouns when concrete ones will do. If you mean 'More people died,' don't say 'Mortality rose.' . . . Don't use adjectives which merely tell us how you want us to feel about the thing you are describing . . . instead of telling us a thing was 'terrible,' describe it so that we'll be terrified . . . Don't use words too big for the subject. Don't say 'infinitely' when you mean 'very;' otherwise you'll have no word left when you want to talk about something really infinite."[49]

Let me share with you another statistic. The average pastor has a working vocabulary of 12,500 words. The average layperson has a working vocabulary of 7,500 words, and of those 7,500 words that the layperson has in his or her vocabulary, 2,500 of those words are related to his or her vocation. So that leaves only 5,000 words that the pastor and the layperson have in common.

Senator Robert Kennedy was a devoted Catholic. Kennedy once went to his priest with a complaint. "The sermons at weekly mass are too difficult to understand," he explained to the priest. His children, whom he regularly took to church, were missing the point. "My kids are pretty bright," Bobby told the priest. "If they don't get the point, other people won't either." Bobby told the clergyman his sermon should be like his own political speeches, simple and clear, going directly to the point. When he realized that he had perhaps been too forceful in expressing his opinion, Kennedy backed off. "I didn't mean to be so intense," he said. "But religion is so important in life. I want my kids to like it. You should not be talking about God up there so much," he said. "I want to know what God is like down here, how he is concerned with what we do here. I want to know how my life should be lived here now." ⁵⁰

Now obviously, dull, abstract preaching is not the special province of our Roman Catholic friends, though I did chuckle when someone shared with me the three great mysteries of the Roman Catholic Church: "One, what is the nature of God? Two, what is the meaning of life? And three, what is it that our priest is talking about?" Believe me, a lot of Protestant laypeople would ask, what is my pastor saying as well? Let's keep our language simple and concise. We also want to keep it concrete and specific. Now what do I mean by concrete? Try to appeal to the five senses—touch, sight, hearing, smell, taste. If you can appeal to the five senses, if you can describe the situation so that we can feel it and taste it and touch it and hear it and so on, then you're being concrete. Otherwise, you're being abstract.

What do I mean by concrete language and imagery? Imagine a stack of one thousand dollar bills. Do you know how tall a stack of one thousand dollar bills would have be to make a billion dollars? It would be 29 feet higher than the Washington monument. Let me put it another way. Let's suppose that I started spending a thousand dollars a day. Suppose I did this every day of the year. Do you know how long it would take me to spend a billion dollars? It would take more than 3000 years. Bill Gates is worth 70 billion dollars. Is that a lot of money?

Make it real so people can see it. Find striking images that impress on the listener the magnitude of what you're trying to describe. For example, there was a story in the newspapers about two boys who were killed in an automobile accident. Drinking and drugs were involved. One of the boys was wearing a tee shirt. On the front of the tee shirt were these words: I'M NOT HERE FOR A LONG TIME. I'M HERE FOR A GOOD TIME.

I used that in a seminar in Chicago. We were in a large ballroom and the kitchen was next door. After the seminar a young worker in the kitchen came out and said "I heard you talking about that fellow in that traffic accident wearing that tee shirt. I have one of those tee shirts at home. I've got some problems I'd like to talk with you about." That image caught his attention. If I had delivered a lecture on the futility of living just for today that would not have caught his attention at all.

Keep your language active and descriptive. Pulpit presentations have a tendency to be passive. A passive sentence is something like this: A wonderful sermon was preached by Brother Jones. That's passive as opposed to: Brother Jones preached a wonderful sermon. That's active. I preached a wonderful sermon. That's bragging. Much preaching is done in the passive voice. I'm not sure why that's true, except that maybe some of us are such nice people that we just don't talk in a direct manner.

Make it active. Make it descriptive. For example, don't say "Somebody walked into the room." That doesn't tell us anything about how they came into the room. Say they sauntered into the room or they skipped into the room or they trudged into the room. Try to say something besides "walked." Try to paint a picture. Help us know how that person came into the room because that's going to tell something about their experience. "He shuffled into the room with his shoulders stooped." Help us to see the total picture. Watch your language.

Watch placement. You've chosen your objective for your sermon, you've chosen your theme, you've developed an outline of how this theme ought to unfold, you've chosen illustrations to fit each of the points. It's time to look at your illustrations and analyze where they would be most effective. You may have to change your outline on the basis of your illustrations because there are some illustrations that just by their very nature, make great climaxes. Some make great introductions. If you're not sensitive to what makes a great climax and what makes a great introduction, you'll rob your preaching of power.

Maintain balance. Let me quote George Sweezy: "Unless there is careful proportioning, a sermon on Romans 5:20 'Where sin abounded grace did much more abound' is likely to have sin abounding through 3/4 of the sermon and grace much less abounding because time ran out."

A common criticism of many pastors is that they are strong on posing the problem, but weak when it comes to solution. Inadequate preparation time is usually the culprit here.

Seek provocative titles. Pastor Mark Sprowl tells about Dr. Donald Macleod, long-time Homiletics professor at Princeton Seminary. Dr. Macleod believed in compelling sermon titles. In fact, he asked students to give their sermon title before beginning each sermon.

Macleod would tell of Mrs. O'Leary who would hop on the Fifth Avenue bus on Sunday morning in Manhattan and pass the great churches along that thoroughfare. As the bus would approach each church, she would eye the sign in front with the sermon title and decide, on the basis of what she read, whether to get off the bus and attend that church. Dr. Macleod's constant refrain was, "Pick a title that will make Mrs. O'Leary get off the bus."

Mindful of that instruction, one of his aspiring preachers mounted the pulpit one morning for his first student sermon. He announced: "The title of my sermon is . . . 'There's a Bomb on the Bus.'" [51]

That's one way to get Mrs. O'Leary off the bus. I have to confess that coming up with a clever, ear- and eye-catching title is very difficult for me. I have tried using the titles of soap operas, playing with headlines from newspapers, etc. I hope you have more success than I at getting Mrs. O'Leary off that bus. A good title can be helpful in enticing new people to visit your church and in helping old members approach worship with anticipation.

Preach for a response. Harry Emerson Fosdick put it this way: "The preacher's business is not merely to discuss repentance but to persuade people to repent; not merely to debate the meaning and possibility of Christian faith, but to produce Christian faith in the lives of his listeners; not merely to talk about the available power of God to bring victory over trouble and temptation, but to send people out from their worship on Sunday with victory in their possession."

Never forget that your primary purpose is to evoke a response in the heart and the life of your people. Augustine defined the preacher's task as *docere, deletare, flectere*—to teach, to delight, to influence. To touch the mind, the heart, the will. [52]

The question you will want to ask as you prepare your message is, "How can I get my congregation to listen to what I am saying and respond in a specific way?" If you aren't seeking for a response, you're not preaching. I'm not talking about an emotional outburst. I'm not talking about people rushing to the altar, although if that happens, that's wonderful. What I want to get away from is the idea that the purpose of preaching is to produce a work of art you can hang on a wall and admire. That's not preaching.

Every once in a while, I have a pastor say to me, "King, I was taught that preaching was an offering to God, and whether anything really happens in the congregation or not is irrelevant." I can't deal with that. I don't believe that is New Testament preaching. To me, preaching is to counsel, to comfort, to convict, to convert, to prod, or to persuade--all those active verbs. Something ought to happen in the life of the person in the pew when preaching takes place.

Kierkegaard compares preachers to swimming coaches who shout instructions to their swimmers but don't think anyone will actually jump in. In fact, as he says, if one were to plunge in to the water and start toward the deep, the coach would be frightened and threatened. [53]

Preaching demands some kind of response. Dr. Joseph Parker once said to a young preacher, "Young man, for the last half hour, you have been trying to get something out of your head instead of something into mine."

As someone has said, "When someone is hungry, they want a meal, not a menu. When they are starving, they want rice, not a recipe." If communication takes place, you have done your job. You're not responsible for changing people; that's the Holy Spirit's job. Your job is to communicate the gospel in such a way that people know in what direction they should go.

Two Greek orators in the fourth century BC supposedly prompted a cry heard among crowds: "When Isocrates speaks, people say, 'How well he speaks!' When Demosthenes speaks, they say, 'Let's march!'"

Keep it simple. Here are two parables. A small girl came home from school one day. Her mother asked how she did. "I was the smartest one in the whole class," she said.

"Really?" asked her mother. "What happened?"

"We wrote on the blackboard," said the little girl proudly. "And I was the only kid in the class who could read my writing."

Second parable: a young man sought out Mark Twain for advice on running for Congress. In response, Twain told the young man a story. It seems there was once a young man who ran for the state legislature. He was so eager to make a good impression that he began to read the dictionary, hoping to improve his vocabulary. It resulted in his speeches becoming so laden with big and obscure words that no one could understand him anymore. One day, the young man was milking a cow and practicing one of his speeches. The cow tired of his endless harangue, kicked him in the jaw and made him bite off the end of his tongue.

"Well!" said the aspiring candidate to Mark Twain. "I guess that put an end to the man's political career."

"Oh, no!" said Twain. "After that, he could use only words of one syllable and it made his speeches so simple and so appealing that he was elected every time."

Use simple, concise sentences. The first law of a boring sermon, how long are the sentences? Rudolf Flesch in *The Art of Plain Talk* insists that clarity increases as sentence length decreases. Be careful about using too many complex ideas.

Reuel Howe listened to hundreds of taped sermons, then he held discussions with many lay people. He reported that the people in the pew complained almost unanimously that sermons often contain too many ideas and those ideas are too complex. If you write out your sermon, don't be afraid of contractions. The *Wall Street Journal* isn't. You'd probably think that of all the newspapers published, the *Journal* would be the most formal, the stuffiest. Not so. One reason why this paper is so easy to read, says one expert, is that you'll find contractions in practically every sentence. This makes for easier reading.

Avoid jargon. It's so easy to pick out the pastor fresh out of seminary. His or her sermons are filled with the jargon of the seminary, and much of it flies over the head of the people in the pew. In the old joke, Jesus asks his disciples, "Who do men say that I am?" They say, "Some say you're Jeremiah, or one of the prophets." Jesus says, "But who do you say that I am?" This time, the apostle John answers and says, "You are the ground of our being, the eschatological manifestation of the kerygma." And Jesus says, "Uh . . . what?"

Be particularly concerned not only about the 50 cent words. Be concerned about even the simplest theological term. This is particularly true if you are trying to reach people with little experience of church. As pastor Rick Warren has said, "The spiritual terminology that Christians are familiar with is just gibberish to unbelievers."

Australian evangelist Alan Walker tells of preaching a sermon early in his ministry titled, "The Cross of Jesus," which took as its text the verse, "God forbid that I should glory in anything save the cross of Jesus Christ." After the service, a young Australian approached Walker and asked if he could borrow his manuscript. Since this hadn't happened to him before, Walker was flattered and gave the manuscript to the young man.

A few days later, this young man returned and brought the manuscript. He said, "I hope you don't mind. But I've underlined all the words that I do not understand. I grew up in a non-Christian home and so I know nothing about Christianity. I've been to a few churches lately to try to learn what the Christian faith is all about."

Walker looked at the manuscript. Every theological word was underlined, and I don't mean words like eschatology and kerygma. For example, "What do you mean by 'in Christ?'" the young man asked Walker. What do you mean by "in Christ?" Everybody understands what it means to be "in Christ," don't they? Give your congregation a quiz next Sunday. Ask them what "salvation" means while you are at it.

I was driving through South Carolina one Sunday morning. It was right after Hurricane Bob had come up the coast, causing lots of havoc. On the radio, I listened to a Southern Baptist pastor tell about an incident that he read about in a newspaper concerning Hurricane Bob.

Two men and a woman were stranded in the ocean by the hurricane. Their boat overturned and they were hanging on to the wreckage. Their radio was gone. Their food was gone. All they could do was to hold on, wait, hope and pray that someone would spot them. It was an exciting story and the pastor told it in wonderful detail. Fortunately, the trio were discovered in the water and were rescued. After telling this story, the pastor turned to his congregation and said, "Now that's what salvation is. When we're totally helpless and can't do anything for ourselves, God reaches down to us and if we're willing, he saves us."

He gave his congregation a simple, concrete example. They could see it and taste it and touch it. In their minds, they could experience what it was to be out there in the ocean clinging to the wreckage, hoping and praying that someone would notice.

Ask this question continuously as you prepare your message, "Who am I trying to impress?" Some pastors are still trying to impress their old Homiletics professor. They are preparing their messages for a class in preaching rather than seeking to deeply influence the people who hear them every Sunday. Again, as Craddock has expressed it, many of us are too aware of those in the balconies observing our performances whom we wish to please or impress. Remember that Kierkegaard was often criticized for lacking dignity and seriousness because he used parable, paradox, irony, humor, etc. But he is still influencing people today, and influencing people is what it is all about.

If in doubt about whether your sermon is too complex for the average lay person, read it to someone else. My wife has always helped me at this point. She always said that she spoke for the common person. I have always made it a practice of reading my message to her before it is delivered or goes into print. Somehow, she's stayed with me nearly 50 years in spite of that.

Air Force General Billy Mitchell always kept an officer at his headquarters to whom he read all his orders. If that officer could understand those orders, he assumed that the other officers could understand them as well. This officer was not particularly bright, but according to Mitchell, he was one of the most useful officers on that staff for that reason. There is an element here of the crucifixion of the self. Some pastors will have to give up a lot of pride to keep it simple. Unless you have a special church, your average listener comprehends on a 6th grade level. Anything higher than a 6th grade level and you're preaching to impress, not to influence.

Be brief. The longest sermon on record was preached by Clinton Lacy of West Richland, Washington, in February of 1955. It took 48 hours and 18 minutes to deliver. On hearing of this accomplishment, someone proposed the adoption of a new Beatitude: "Blessed is the preacher whose train of thought has a caboose."

"Begin at the beginning," the king said gravely in Lewis Carroll's, *Alice's Adventures in Wonderland*, "and go until you come to the end, then stop." Good advice.

A political candidate had been speaking for 40 minutes to an increasingly impatient audience and was finally making his closing remarks. Waving his arms for emphasis, he said in a booming and forceful voice, "We need reform! We need educational reform! We need housing reform! We need tax reform! We need …" and someone in the audience yelled, "Chloroform!" Obviously this speaker was in violation of the MEGO factor: "My Eyes Glaze Over."

The shortest inaugural address was George Washington's. He went first. He kept it brief. We've gone downhill ever since. Washington's address was 135 words. The longest was William Henry Harrison's address in 1941. It was a 2 hour, 9,000 words speech delivered during a freezing wind. A month later, he was dead of pneumonia. A lesson, perhaps?

As it has often been noted, the Ten Commandments contain only 297 words. The Bill of Rights is stated in 463 words. Lincoln's Gettysburg Address contains only 266 words. Studies show that most people can concentrate on a given subject for only 6 minutes at a stretch because of distractions.

A wise preacher might strive to package his or her message in 6 minute gulps or segments. Three 6 minute gulps or points, a 1 minute introduction and a 1 minute conclusion and "Voila!" –the tried and true 20-minute sermon. Actually, the truly memorable message might be 8 minutes long with a 1 minute introduction and a 1 minute conclusion around a 6 minute gulp.

I know a marvelous pastor who would be so much more effective if he pared down his 30 minute sermon to 15 minutes. He could use the same material but pare it down to a concise, economical, hard-hitting, *Reader's Digest* version. His stock with his congregation would rise immensely. Should every sermon be 15 minutes in length? Of course not. I read somewhere that Pastor Rob Bell sometimes preaches 100-minute sermons. Some preachers can preach for an extended time and still be brief. Henry Ward Beecher once said, "The true way to shorten a sermon is to make it more interesting," and that's true. But as someone has said, "No sermon is entirely bad if it's short enough."

Watch about having too many "points" in a propositional message. A communication school did a study of chess players and found that the human brain can only retain about five things without memory loss. If that is true of chess players . . . ?

In the back of this book is a list of shifting paradigms for ministry in the 21st century. You might want to study that list very carefully. One of those shifting paradigms is: Old Paradigm, Great Preacher; New Paradigm, Effective Communicator.

Work on your conclusion. Charles Osgood, TV anchor on CBS, confesses that he often writes the last line of a speech first. Since the last thing you say is what your audience is most likely to remember, your conclusion is important. I have heard many sermons saved by a strong conclusion. Spend nearly as much time on it as your introduction.

Make sure your sermon is Good News. Now what do I mean by that? Brought up in the hills of East Tennessee, I grew up in a church believing that you could always tell a Christian by what he didn't do. That is, if he didn't smoke, or drink, or chew, he was probably a Christian. I don't smoke, drink or chew, but there's no virtue in that. It's just the way I was raised.

One of my favorite stories is about a little boy in Sunday School making a drawing. His teacher asks, "Johnny, what are you drawing?"

He says "Oh, I'm drawing a saloon and this is a cowboy and he's going into the saloon." The teacher looks a little shocked. He says, "Oh don't worry teacher he's not going into the saloon to drink; he's going in there to shoot somebody."

That was the way I was brought up. It's better to shoot somebody than to take a drink. I don't drink and I'm thankful for that, but that's hardly the content of the Gospel. And most certainly negative, moralistic preaching will not fly today.

People have changed. It does no good to beat them over the head with moralistic diatribes. In a harshly disciplined society with lots of rules, regulations and punishment, there was a bountiful supply of free-floating guilt that a preacher could use for a short-term behavioral change. But in a society in which people have been brought up permissively, they don't even feel guilty about things they ought to feel guilty about. You don't have that free-floating guilt to draw on. What you have to do if you want to effect behavioral change is to paint a positive picture that is so appealing that folks say, "I've got to have that." That's the only way long-term change takes place.

Let me give you a quick example. Several years ago there was an article in the newspapers about the Daytona 500. They were interviewing a guy who was a groupie of stock car drivers. He loves stock car racing and he follows these stock car drivers everywhere. He said, "I really used to love to go to Daytona. Those stock car drivers were party animals. We'd get there a week early, and it would just be party after party, and these guys would be up all night partying and carousing. They were up 'til dawn having a great time. I just loved it."

He said, "It's no fun going to Daytona anymore. These same stock car drivers are going to bed early and getting up at dawn and jogging on the beach."

What changed? Did the drivers go home to their Baptist or Methodist church and the preacher beat them over the head about their carousing lifestyle? No. Somebody's painted a picture in our society of a disciplined life where you can stay younger longer and you can keep your energy level and your reflexes longer. Many people have been attracted to that lifestyle. I believe that's the most effective kind of preaching today. If I was going to talk about faithfulness in marriage, I wouldn't beat people over the head with the "Thou shalt nots." I'd point to an older couple sitting down front who've been married 50 years and still holding hands, and I'd tell my young couples, "Do you want that kind of joy in your old age? It comes out of being faithful and loving to each other."

When moralism creeps into sermons, it's generally in the choice of illustrations. And it's usually because somebody pulled in an illustration from a long time ago when you could use guilt to change people. I'm not saying don't make people feel guilty. I'm not saying that at all. There are things people ought to feel guilty about. Part of the task of the preacher is to afflict the comfortable. I don't have any problem with that. I'm just saying that if you want real change to take place, seek to build a positive message that is so attractive that people are led to desire that change.

Invite feedback. A national sportscaster told of his frustration when some of his listeners shared their feeling that he was too negative in his comments during the telecasts of certain games. Surely, he wasn't guilty of this, he thought. In order to test it out, he arranged for an office stenographer to take down every word he uttered at the next event he broadcast. He discovered how frequently he was indeed unnecessarily critical. He wouldn't have known it, however, if he hadn't asked for feedback.

When *U.S. Catholic* asked its readers to suggest ideas to improve preaching in Roman Catholic churches, a rich and surprising group of answers emerged. For example, 69% said that good sermons should be applauded. I like that. A majority replied that lay people should be allowed to preach. Another response was that churches should have the nerve to publish a schedule of who preaches at each mass so that parishioners could follow their favorites. I thought that was kind of interesting. A majority of 62% believed that there should be sermons about money, but the bulk of those replying felt that once a year was enough. While 63% said that they are frequently or always satisfied with the Sunday sermon they hear, 83% do not want the sermon to stretch beyond 20 minutes. And finally, and most daring of all, 73% of the parishioners would like to have a pew card on which they could comment on individual sermons.

Many of us do not really like feedback. Preaching is a very personal experience and we are very sensitive about how our sermons are received. If we are to keep growing, however, feedback is essential.

Keep growing spiritually and intellectually. I've mentioned that George Buttrick made it a practice to read at least one book every week. That's a good discipline to follow if you can find the time. Discipline is, of course, the key. Let me say this about that: clergy are the happiest occupational group—followed by psychologists, artists and entertainers. But my guess is that there are few people unhappier than an undisciplined pastor.

Keep growing, for heaven's sake. Do it for Christ. Do it for the church. It makes a difference in the freshness of preaching if the pastor is a continuing student. Do it for yourself. People who keep alert intellectually, age better. The brain is like a muscle in that respect. You can keep it toned by intellectual stimulation. Don't get into the habit of coasting mentally. If you are coasting, you are going downhill. If you do not have a few minutes set aside for Bible study each day, you are making a big mistake. But, don't stop there. Read the best works in psychology, history, sports, etc.

Make more time by utilizing your laity. This is not a workshop on time management, nevertheless, I get weary of pastors saying to me, "I don't have enough time for sermon preparation."

Go back and read Scott Peck's book *A Road Less Traveled*. Remember that scene where, as a young psychiatrist, he finds himself spending far more time with his patients than the other therapists do? They are all leaving at 5:00 and he's working late into the evening. Pretty soon, he is filled with resentment. He goes to the senior member of the staff to express his distress and to see if perhaps he could get his caseload lightened.

The older doctor listens patiently and then says simply, "Well, Scott, I can see you have a problem." Then he says nothing more.

"I know I have a problem," Peck responded. "What should I do?"

"You're not listening to me, Scott," said the older doctor, "I'm agreeing with you, you have a problem."

"I know I have a problem," said Peck, "That's why I'm here! What should I do?"

"You're not listening to me Scott," said the older doctor, "you have a problem."

At that, Peck shot out of the office, slamming the door behind him. He hated that so-and-so for months after that . . . until it slowly dawned on him that the older doctor was right. This was his problem. Only he could solve it. He would have to establish some priorities. He would have to take the responsibility for making those choices upon himself. Nobody else could do it for him.

If top-notch preaching is truly one of your priorities, it must get priority of time. That means utilization of your laity. That is your main job as pastor anyway. The highest compliment you can pay a lay person is to ask him or her to perform a meaningful ministry. Anything you do that can be turned over to a lay person is cheating someone in your church spiritually. It is also cheating your entire congregation every week if it takes away time for your sermon preparation.

Depend on God. You have been ordained. Great. In the book of Jonah, God ordained a whale, a worm, a gourd and a sultry east wind. In the story of Balaam, God spoke through a donkey. Ordination in and of itself will not make you a great preacher.

Some scholars have suggested that when King George II stood for the Hallelujah Chorus in that famous event that we memorialize each Christmas and Easter, it was because he thought the Hallelujah chorus was a tribute to him. "And He shall reign forever and ever!"

My favorite example is the old tuba player in the Burlesque show who would play while the audience applauded wildly. Behind him, stripper Gypsy Rose Lee was doing her thing, but the old tuba player thought they were applauding him.

In one of the old Marks Brothers' films, Harpo Marks is leaning against the corner of a large bank. He's asked by a policeman if he thinks he's propping up the bank or something. Harpo smiles and nods. He is told to move on. He does, and the bank collapses.

Some pastors are afraid to take a vacation. They're afraid that their church will collapse while they are gone. "What do you think we are doing here, propping up God or something?" asks Ian Pitt Thomas. If he had to, God could manage without us. Our help comes from God alone. Keep your spiritual life alive and fresh. I have taken that for granted in this book. That does not mean that it is not critical.

These are the keys to effective preaching. I am trusting that you will make effective use of them. Let me conclude this section by suggesting that you set some goals for your preaching. There is an old story of a young preacher who asked his mentor following his first sermon, "Well, will that do?"

His mentor asked, "Do what?" What are some things you hope to achieve with your preaching? Let me suggest a few and then you add to my list. Some of you will preach the best sermon you have ever preached this Sunday if you will simply measure your message according to these goals.

1. **Do I have something I really must say?**

2. **Will everyone know what I have said when I finish?**

3. **Will they believe that I meant what I said?**

4. **Will they remember what I say?**

5. **Is what I am saying relevant to the real needs of my people?**

6. **Could a life be changed by my message?**

7. **Is my message faithful to the scripture as best I can prayerfully understand it?**

8. **Did my message move toward a celebration?**

Using Humor in the Pulpit

I have had many pastors--including pastors who are now leading lights in their denominations—who have told me this section of the workshop on using humor changed their whole approach to preaching. I was even invited to present these tips for using humor in a large gathering of Jewish rabbis—and, golly, they invented humor. And so I offer it to you. Use it as you will. Many of the examples are dated, but the principles are timeless. King Duncan

At one time I was a member of the National Speakers Association, a remarkable organization that counts among its members such outstanding professional speakers as Zig Ziglar, Tony Robbins, Art Linkletter, etc.—a veritable Who's Who in the world of professional speaking.

We had a truism in NSA: you use humor only . . . if you want to get paid. In other words, you may be the leading expert in your field, you may have a mesmerizing voice which you have trained to be an amazing tool—but, if you do not hold people's interest, there's no reason for you to be on the platform. Humor is the best tool we have for holding people's interest. You're not a professional speaker. What has becoming proficient in the use of humor got to do with preaching?

I am thoroughly convinced that humor is also the most effective single tool in the preacher's workshop. I am convinced that you use humor only . . . if you want to keep people coming back for more. "A boring speaker," says Eric Shiveley, "is one who doesn't know when to quip."

It is said that the actor Edmund Gwenn's last words were, "Dying is easy, comedy is difficult." Comedy, or in our case, humor is difficult. However, there is no better device for involving the congregation in a sermon than a good chuckle. Some pastors use humor prolifically and with great effectiveness.

There was a well-known pastor in southern California who used a joke near the end of every sermon. His people eagerly awaited for that piece of humor. I'm not sure I would recommend that to everyone. That was California, after all.

I love Californians. That's one of my favorite places to do workshops. They pride themselves on being different. I've heard there's a sign as you leave California and go into Arizona saying, "You are now leaving California; resume normal behavior."

Let me give you some practical, straight-forward reasons why you probably should be using more humor in your preaching. Notice I didn't say jokes. Fred Craddock says you probably shouldn't use jokes in preaching. And you shouldn't . . . if you're Fred Craddock. Craddock's a genius and a masterful user of humor. He doesn't need other people's material to be funny.

But the joke is only one form of humor--and there are times when even a joke can be very useful--though I will agree with Craddock that there are many types of humor that can be more effective in preaching.

But why should you use humor at all? I'm going to list seven reasons.

Humor maintains interest. People perk up their ears when you're using humor. We don't have a more dialogical tool than humor. Unless you're in a church where people say things like, "Praise the Lord" . . . "Preach on" . . . and, from time to time . . . "Help him, Jesus," laughter is about the only time you may know your folks are alive.

Humor helps promote togetherness. People are 30 times more likely to laugh in groups than alone. When people laugh, they feel closer together. You notice that on a church retreat. People sit out on the front porch of the lodge and they are telling stories and laughing. That's a great part of Christian fellowship. There's no reason why such togetherness can't take place in the worship.

Humor confirms our common humanity. Humor is a sign of grace. I could do a whole workshop on that. Humor confirms the fact that all of us are weak, none of us is perfect. A pompous person can't use humor because they have never learned to laugh at themselves or at their situation.

Humor builds rapport. When you help people laugh they feel warmer toward you. Why else would a guest preacher tell jokes at the beginning of his or her message? He, or she, is seeking to build rapport.

Humor affirms your humanity. The fact that you are an ordained minister of the gospel puts you on a pedestal, as far as your folks are concerned. That's true in any tradition. We Protestants have been talking about the priesthood of believers for 400 years, and nobody believes it for a second. As far as lay people are concerned, there are men and women and clergy. When you use humor, it's a way of helping you get off the pedestal for a few minutes and making people feel that they can relate to you one-on-one.

Conversely, the ability to use humor enhances your image. We respect people today who can use humor. Corporations bring in professional comedians to teach their executives how to use humor because it's recognized that the ability to use humor is a leadership skill. It has to do with a particular operational style.

A study was done of paintings of corporate and government leaders over the last century. In the early days, corporate and government leaders were always portrayed in paintings as being stern, aloof and cold. They would always sit back in their chair and stare into the distance. Today, if you look at a picture of a government or corporate leader they're leaning toward you and their face shows warmth. The ability to use humor is part of that more informal, dialogical, conversational style that says we're all in this together.

You say, "Well, that's not me." Then, work on it. Authority-based preaching is dead. You need to reach out to people with grace . . . and love . . . and humor. Abraham Lincoln was a master in the use of humor. When challenged to a duel by a southern gentleman, he accepted under the condition he could pick the weapon and the location. After the gentleman accepted those conditions, Lincoln responded, "Cow dung at five feet." You can guess the result.

And there is one more reason why you ought to be using humor in your preaching--the most important reason of all.

Jesus did it. I know, the New Testament doesn't say that he used humor, but anyone familiar with the devices of humor knows he did. He told puns. Puns have been described as the lowest form of humor, but that didn't deter him. For example, he spoke of straining at a gnat and swallowing a camel. "You blind guides! You strain at a gnat (*galma*) but swallow a camel (*gama*)." It's a pun, a clever play on words. His listeners would have undoubtedly chuckled [or groaned] as we normally do with a pun.

He used wild exaggeration—which is one of the prime ingredients in the use of humor. He talked about getting a speck out of your neighbor's eye while you have a 2' x 4' sticking out of your eye. That's absurd imagery. But even some of the things he said which we don't think of as funny contain humorous elements.

I wish I could go back and hear him tell the stories in Luke 15. For example, the woman who loses a coin and sweeps out her whole house to find that one lost coin. Then what does she do? She throws a party and invites all her neighbors. Surely the party cost more than that one lost coin. Jesus gives us a picture of a God who, in His love and grace, is so extravagant that He doesn't bother to calculate the bills.

Or the parable of the ninety and nine. The shepherd's out there with 100 sheep. One goes astray, and he goes to find the one lost sheep. What does he do with the ninety and nine? Where does he leave them? We think of the old gospel song and picture him leaving them in "the shelter of the fold," but that's not what the scripture says. It says he left them in the wilderness. Now if any shepherds were standing around, they would say, "That's not very good shepherding—leaving 99 sheep unprotected in the wilderness while you go find one that's gone astray."

But Jesus is deliberately expressing truth through outrageous language, and I've got a feeling if we had been there, we would have been standing around with that group of men listening to Jesus and from to time we would have roared with laughter. Then he would have made his point after he had us all softened up. That was the way Jesus taught.

He used hyperbole after hyperbole. There was the guy who owed his boss a million dollars and the boss forgives him. But he can't forgive another guy who owes him 100 dollars. The hyperbole is so striking, it's hilarious, but that was Jesus' method. Think about a camel trying to squeeze through a needle's eye. It is ludicrous.

The critics called Christ a wine bibber and a glutton. He was having far too much fun in life. Jesus was a party lover who loved to be with people, and obviously people were laughing the whole time they were around him. I just wish we could go back and hear him live.

Even when he said to Nicodemus that he must be born all over again. We've sanitized that expression and turned that into a very somber doctrine, but old Nicodemus took it literally. He questioned how he could go back into his mother's womb and be born all over.

Personally, I think Jesus meant for him to take it literally. I think Jesus was saying to Nicodemus, "Look friend, you're a product of your culture. I am bringing in a new way of living and loving that for you to even understand it, you would have to go back into your mother's womb and be born all over again."

I suspect that Jesus is saying the same thing to us. But we've ritualized it and made it safe so it doesn't really require any great change out of us at all.

Oops, I'm on my soapbox. Sorry. But I believe if we could go back and listen with fresh ears to Jesus as a good Jewish story-teller who used the devices of humor to speak into being a new kingdom, it would change our lives. It was said of him in Mark 12:37, "The large crowd listened to Jesus with delight." (NIV)

I believe that if we are going to change lives today, we need also to be storytellers who use humor to bring the kingdom alive for our generation.

The Midrash tells a number of stories about Abraham. Some of them are fanciful and even humorous. Perhaps best known is the legend that Abraham's father, Terach, was an idol-maker, and one night Abraham, entrusted to watch over the workshop, smashed all his father's idols. In the morning, his father angrily upbraided him. "What have you done to my livelihood?"

Abraham calmly replied, "It wasn't me. The idols had a fight with each other."

Enraged, Terach said, "What are you talking about? They can't fight with each other. They are made of wood and stone!"

Abraham nodded and asked, "Then why, Father, do you worship them?"

That's both humorous and profound at the same time.

Twenty tips for using humor in preaching "Analyzing humor is like dissecting a frog. Few people are interested and the frog dies in the process." -- E. B. White

I hear two objections from pastors when I try to get them to use humor in their preaching. The first is that "humor trivializes the message."

Several years ago, I received a letter from a pastor in which he said, "King, I think perhaps some of the stories you choose for *Dynamic Preaching* are a little too funny." He said, "Now don't get me wrong. A story that brings a smile to the faces of the congregation can be very helpful, but when people break out in riotous laughter, you've gone too far."

I thought to myself, "Wow, he must be great at telling these stories." But he was serious.

I wrote him back and said: "Do you know what trivializes the message? It is when a pastor has been droning on for 20 or 25 minutes and nobody has any idea what he or she has said. Why? Because they're not listening. What could trivialize a message more than that?"

Charles Spurgeon once said, "I'd rather have them laughing than have them sleeping." Spurgeon was well known for his sense of humor. In fact, a lady criticized Spurgeon for his use of humor and Spurgeon replied, "My dear, you don't know how much I hold back."

Martin Luther said that a sense of humor was the second most desirable characteristic in a pastor. Martin Luther said on one occasion, "If you're not allowed to laugh in heaven, I don't want to go there."

Lee Tuttle, in his study of pulpit giants said that the most universal characteristic of these great preachers was their great sense of humor. Obviously, I don't believe humor trivializes the message.

The second objection I hear from pastors about using humor in the pulpit is, "King, I just can't tell a joke." Every once in a while, I'll run into a pastor who can't tell a joke. You know who you are.

Well, anyone can tell a joke. But it takes work. This book is designed to be very basic. It is primarily for those who may feel uncomfortable using humor in the pulpit. That was once true of me. I'm very left-brained, analytical, as I've already noted. Humor does not come naturally for me. I have to work at being humorous, but I believe any pastor can be effective using humor by just following a few simple rules.

Acknowledge that humor is a skill. That is, there are no born comedians. It is true that each of us is born with certain aptitudes, among these may be the ability to use humor. Some are more gifted than others. But, like any aptitude, a sense of humor can be developed. And the ability to use humor is a skill that can be learned.

Make a humor commitment. Like anything else in the world, if you're going to be good at it, you have to make a commitment to using humor. Set goals for yourself: "Hey, I'm going to be the best user of humor in my part of the country by this time next year." Make that kind of commitment and stick with it.

I had a close friend who is now with God. He was known as a great user of humor. He was a pastor. When there was a big church event or conference, he would be called on to be the master of ceremonies. He was terrific. I would hear folks say, "Ah, he's just a natural. It's a gift he has."

You don't know how many nights my friend stayed up to watch the late night comics and write down every one of their jokes, diagramming them to learn what made them funny. He worked at that all of his adult life nearly. And he became a pro.

One of my favorite preachers, mega-church pastor Mike Slaughter, says that when he started preaching, he didn't study preachers. He studied comedians! He calls Richard Pryor and Bill Cosby two of his mentors. He figured that anyone who could talk for an hour and have people pay $75 a head to hear them had to have something going on. He says that anytime he has an opportunity to watch a comedy special on television, he watches it and studies everything the comedian does. "It's not that I want to be funny," he says. "I simply want to learn more about engaging an audience." [54]

Here's the reason you need to make a commitment. A pastor who is uncomfortable using humor will tell a piece of humor, and perhaps it will bomb. The comedians call it dying, and, boy, that's how it feels (not that it's ever happened to me. Ha, ha). And so the tendency is to say, "I'll never use a piece of humor again in a sermon."

Friend, everybody who uses humor dies from time to time. Leno and Letterman sometimes use jokes that absolutely stink. That's just part of the process. But every once in a while, they will knock one out of the park, and it more than makes up for the strikeouts (pardon the mixed metaphors). But it requires a real commitment.

Seek quality material. Keep your eyes and ears open all the time for humorous things around you. And they are out there. You have to be looking for them.

My wife and I bought a white car sometime back. I had no idea there were so many white cars on the road until we bought that car. Have you had that experience? I think most of us have. You buy a Ford and suddenly realize how many people drive Fords. That's the way it is with humor. There is so much humor in this world, but unless you cue your brain into looking for it, it won't be obvious.

Consider your audience. For example, I would never try to tell jokes to teenagers. There are some teenagers who would rather die than laugh at an adult's jokes. It's an affront to them. So I don't even try. I try to find humor in their experience and build on that.

Women laugh at different things than men do. Try never to have an all-male audience if you can help it. Male audiences tend to be a little stiffer than female audiences. Women laugh more than men. The old stereotype is that women don't have a sense of humor. In Mark Twain's *Diary of Adam and Eve*, Eve was created without a sense of humor. That was the old stereotype. But studies of actual audiences show that women are less inhibited than men are, and women laugh a lot more.

Having said that, it is also true that women laugh at different things than men do. Women's humor tends to be more personal, less competitive. There's a difference, and you need to be sensitive to that difference. Choose your humor according to the demographics of the group to which you are speaking.

Write the piece of humor in your own words. It's part of making the humor your own.

Go slow. That is, don't try to be Jay Leno [fill in the name of your favorite comedian] overnight. Leno didn't become Leno overnight. It's like any other skill. It takes time.

Think "brief." A joke, or nearly any piece of humor, should be told in as few words as possible. Anything that you can cut out, do. Of course, you can't cut out the essential elements.

I heard about a movie theater in Europe that was showing an American movie. The manager decided it was too long so he cut out what he thought was unessential—the music. The movie was *The Sound of Music*. He cut it to 7-1/2 minutes.

You can't cut out what's essential to the joke, but do make it as brief as possible. That way, the punch line has more punch.

Try to slip in something humorous every time you step into the pulpit. Why? Because you want to build a **laughter expectancy**. People laugh more when they are primed for laughter. Every comic understands this to be their greatest asset. If you have a reputation for making people laugh, they come ready to laugh, and they are going to laugh more than they would have laughed if they hadn't been primed by that expectation.

Now, you're not a comic, but you do want to use some of the skills that the great comics use. Congregations have to be trained to respond to humor. And they can be. But sometimes it's difficult. After all, some people haven't laughed in church in 20 years. So, you're going to have to train them. You do that by starting immediately to slip in a piece of humor every chance you get.

Be yourself. You cannot deliver humor in a stained-glass pulpit voice. If you do, there are two jokes going on, and one is on you. Be yourself. The best humor grows out of your personality.

Make sure you know the punch line. I'm serious. When pastors blow a good story, it's because they mess up the punch line, and there's no excuse for that. There are some people who have difficulty at this point. I've got to tell you a story from the past and I hope if you are a younger pastor, you can relate.

There was once a U.S. Senator named Scoop Jackson. Scoop was a Senator from the state of Washington. He was a fine Senator, but he had a terrible reputation for blowing punch lines.

One night, Scoop was at a cocktail party in Washington, D. C and he overheard two men telling a joke. This was right after Watergate, just after Richard Nixon had resigned from the presidency and Gerald Ford had become president. The first thing Ford did was pardon Nixon for his crimes. The joke went something like this:

After he was no longer President, Richard Nixon came back to the White House one night to retrieve some of his papers. He was feeling around in the dark in the White House and he bumped into Gerry Ford. Richard Nixon said, "Oh, pardon me."

Gerry Ford's response was, "I already have."

Now that was the joke. It was funny back then. Scoop Jackson overheard that conversation and thought, "Hey, I've got to give a speech in Seattle tomorrow night, and I'll start off with that joke." So Scoop Jackson gets up there and says,

"Richard Nixon came back to the White House; he was groping around in the dark and ran into Gerry Ford, and he said 'Oh, *excuse me.*'"

Now what do you do at that point? He was supposed to say, "Oh, pardon me" and he said, "Oh, excuse me." There is no way to retrieve that story. He blew the punch line. So write down the punch line ten times before you ever go into the pulpit. Make sure you know it backwards and forwards. This brings me to the next tip:

Rehearse, rehearse, rehearse. Before you go into the pulpit and a tell humorous piece of material, tell it to your spouse, tell it to your children, tell it to the mail carrier, tell it to everybody you can before you get in the pulpit. You say, "Well, King, won't that take the edge off it? I don't want my spouse to hear it. He or she is part of the congregation. I want him or her to laugh too."

I don't care. You need to rehearse a joke before you tell it publicly. I promise you, it will be worth the effort.

Use pauses. When comedians talk about timing, all they are talking about is the effective use of the pause. For example, before you give a punch line, there ought to be a momentary pause to allow the congregation to be set up for it. And there ought to always be a pause after a punch line to give people time to laugh.

You've seen it happen. When pastors are uncomfortable using humor, what they'll do is tell a joke and then hurry right on because they're afraid nobody will laugh. They cover themselves by going on to the next part. And they wonder why nobody laughs. It's because they didn't give their listeners an opportunity to laugh.

The pros wait. Comedian Jack Benny was famous for his long pauses. The mugger would say, "Your money or your life," and Benny, who was famous for being stingy, would pause for 30 whole seconds before he'd say, "I'm thinking. I'm thinking."

A full 30 seconds. That's a lifetime in front of an audience. But laughter would be building the whole time. Practice pausing.

Remember the rule of threes. Humor is almost always done according to the rule of threes. That is, a rabbi, a minister, and a priest went out one day--that's a clue that a funny story is coming. It's almost always three of something.

Humorists are almost superstitious about this. Notice what happens in comedies on television. If you see something funny happen once, then you'll see it happen twice. Finally, you can count on it happening a third time, because humorists believe there's something about threes that makes a humorous story funnier.

Use Callbacks. A callback is a reference a comedian makes to an earlier joke in a set. If something you said got a good laugh, reference it again later in the message. If something dramatic or

167

extraordinary happened earlier in the service, a humorous reference to it in the message can have the same effect.

Understand that real-life humor is better than jokes. If something funny happens to you, tell it. It will be a lot funnier than any joke you'll ever get out of a joke book.

Humorous anecdotes are safer than jokes. Jokes travel very fast. You tell a joke and think nobody's heard it, but you're going to be surprised. If it's a good joke, somebody in that congregation has heard it. It's very hard to tell a joke nobody's heard before. Sometimes, you can still get away with it, but anecdotes are safer.

The second reason for using anecdotes rather than jokes is that there's less pressure when you tell a humorous anecdote. That is, if you tell a joke and nobody laughs, it's painful for both you and the congregation. But you can tell an anecdote that makes your point, and if people laugh it's a bonus. It can still be a good story without getting a boisterous laugh. Let me give you a quick example of a humorous anecdote. This is something I got out of a psychology text.

It's a true story of a gifted child three years old named Jonathan who had a rather dominant personality. Jonathan's parents take him to a restaurant. The waitress asks, "Jonathan, what would you like?"

Jonathan says, "I'd like a grilled cheese sandwich."

The waitress says, "I'm sorry, we don't serve grilled cheese sandwiches."

Jonathan says, "You have bread, don't you?"

She says, "Yes."

He says, "You have cheese, don't you?"

She says, "Yes."

He says, "You have a grill, don't you?"

She says, "Yes."

Jonathan says, "I'll have a grilled cheese sandwich." Imagine . . . a three-year-old child.

The waitress says, "Okay, Jonathan, I'll go see if the chef will fix you a grilled cheese sandwich."

She comes back in a few minutes and says, "Yes, Jonathan, the chef said he would fix you a grilled cheese sandwich . . . . I forgot to ask you want you want to drink."

Jonathan says, "I'll have a milkshake."

She's ready for him this time. She says, "Now Jonathan, your parents have probably already told you we don't serve milkshakes . . . Now it is true we have milk, and it is true we have ice cream . . . But we don't have any syrup."

Jonathan says, "You own a car, don't you?"

Now I read that and I nearly fell out of my chair. That's hilarious to me. But it's still a good story even if I tell it and nobody laughs. It is not a joke that depends on people laughing. It still makes the point about different personality styles. So humorous anecdotes are a little safer for the pulpit plus they're more real.

Jokes are public domain and may not be copyrighted. Every once in a while, a pastor will ask me, "King, should I always give credit when I'm telling a joke?" No, jokes are public domain. You don't even have to give credit for them. You do need to tell a joke in your own words. And you can't copy somebody else's joke book and publish it as your own. But any individual joke is in the public domain. Just go ahead and tell it and enjoy it.

Put the punch line as close to the end as possible. That's where it belongs. That's what gives it punch.

This seems like a strange thing to say but "despise not old and dumb jokes." That is, remember your task is to illustrate. And if you're telling a story that makes people listen more intently to what you're saying, go for it, even if you know it is a nugget from days gone by.

Why do I say this? I learned a lesson sometime back. I went to a very large, sophisticated, suburban church and snuck in the back because I knew the pastor and I didn't want to be too obvious about being there. He started off with an old, old joke. It's the old story about the pastor who owned a horse that he trained to respond to

"Praise the Lord" rather than "Giddy-up," and "Amen" rather than "Whoa." I can see you grimacing. Let me tell it in condensed form.

A pastor owned a horse and instead of training it to respond to "Giddy-up" he said, "Praise the Lord," and to get it to stop he said "Amen." A lay person bought the horse and the pastor told him, "You're going to have to remember to say 'Praise the Lord' to get him to go and 'Amen' if you want him to stop."

The fellow said "I can remember that." So he buys the horse and says "Giddy-up, horse," and the horse doesn't budge, and he finally remembers and says, "Praise the Lord" and the horse starts galloping along and keeps galloping faster and faster, but he can't remember how to stop it, and he pulls back on the reins and says, "Whoa, horse, whoa." It doesn't do any good. By the time he gets almost to the edge of a cliff, he remembers to say, "Amen." The horse comes to a stop right on the edge, and the man takes out his handkerchief, wipes his brow and says, "Praise the Lord."

That's an old, old joke. The pastor of this large church started off with this story. I was sitting there thinking to myself, "Why in the world is he bringing out that old chestnut?" I'm starting to get embarrassed in his behalf. But when he got to that final, "Praise the Lord," and we watched that guy go off the cliff in our minds, I couldn't believe it. That congregation went crazy. People just roared, children were bouncing back and forth on the back of the pews and teenagers were sitting up listening; old folks were punching each other in the ribs. That congregation went crazy. And then he looked over the pulpit and said, "This morning we're going to talk about some ways we can praise the Lord."

Now was that effective? It was. And it taught me a lesson. When you're into humor, really into humor, you can become jaded. You can move to a level of sophistication that most of your lay folks have not attained. And again, if a story makes your point, if it gets your sermon off and moving, then it's a good story. So don't assume everybody has heard it. Of course, the nice thing about old jokes is when young people come along, it's a new story for them. And the old folks enjoy hearing these golden oldies again. It's a form of nostalgia. So if it makes your point, don't just reject it because it's one you've heard several times. Your lay people might not have heard it at all. I make that point just because of that experience. Remember, you are not the final judge of whether something is funny or not.

In 1978, *Psychology Today* magazine did a humor survey in which 14,500 readers rated 30 jokes. Not surprisingly, different people laughed at different things. Every single joke, it was reported, had a substantial number of fans who rated it very funny, but another group dismissed it as not funny at all. Different strokes for different folks. Even what may seem to you to be a dumb joke may be wonderfully effective—if it makes your point.

The best form of humor for the pastor is self-deprecating humor. If you can make fun of yourself, that's the best kind of humor for a pastor. Why? Because as we've already noted, it takes you off the pedestal. People can relate to you and feel like, hey this is somebody I can talk to. Humor and humility come from the same root word, as does *humus*, dirt.

Now I've had a couple of very shy pastors say to me, "King, if I use self-deprecating humor won't people look down on me?" I say to those pastors, no, it works the other way. In today's society, we recognize that the person who can make fun of himself or herself probably has a high sense of self-esteem. If you can make fun of yourself, at your own dumb mistakes—and who hasn't made a dumb mistake along the way?—if you can tell it and make fun of yourself, that will endear you to your people more than anything else you do.

Ronald Reagan taught us that. Reagan was a master at self-deprecating humor. They called him the Teflon president. Why? Because anything that was aimed at him, he deflected by using humor.

Walter Mondale accused him of government by amnesia. Reagan's response: "I resent that remark about me having amnesia. I wish I could remember who said it."

The White House reporters were giving him a rough time about his leisurely work habits. Reagan comes out of the oval office and says, "Fellows, I want you to know I've been in there burning the mid-day oil."

He said, "Someday there'll be a sign over the oval office: Ronald Reagan slept here."

Now what do you do with somebody who can take any criticism and turn it into humor? Most political strategists say the election between Reagan and Mondale was over as soon as Reagan used that quip, "I will not take advantage of my opponent's relative youth and inexperience." You never heard the age issue mentioned again.

Of course, Reagan had no qualms about making light of his age. "They don't ask me how old I am," he said on one occasion, "they just carbon-date me."

He and Nancy were guests on *Good Morning America* years ago. Nancy was close to the edge of the stage and fell off. Immediately, people rushed to her aid while the president watched. Knowing she was alright, he looked at her and said, "Nancy, I told you not to fall off the platform unless I wasn't getting any applause."

It's impossible to dislike a person who can so effectively laugh at himself. Self-deprecating humor is a powerful instrument in the hands of any leader.

There have been other Presidents who could have been helped by self-deprecating humor, but couldn't pull it off.

Jimmy Carter had difficulty making fun of himself. He did try. On one occasion he sought to defuse all the cracks about his wide and toothy grin. At a speech he told the audience, "My tax return is coming out okay. The only thing the IRS questioned was a six hundred dollar bill for toothpaste." [55]

I love Jimmy Carter. He's one of the finest men in this country. But humor did not come easily for him. If Jimmy Carter made fun of somebody, he made fun of the press. He'd come out of the Oval Office and say, "Fellows, I don't have anything important to say today. You can put away your crayons." You don't do that with the Washington press.

Richard Nixon couldn't make fun of himself. We wouldn't have had Watergate if he could. It wasn't Nixon's politics that defeated him; it was his personality. If he had been the kind of person who could laugh at his own mistakes, we would never have had Watergate.

Lyndon Johnson, bless his heart, couldn't make fun of himself. He had this inflated ego, so when the students protested the war in Vietnam, Johnson hid away in the White House. He couldn't handle the criticism.

John Kennedy could. They were giving Kennedy a hard time in the election about coming from such a wealthy family and Kennedy said, "You don't know how stingy my daddy is. He told me not to buy a single vote more than necessary . . . He said he wasn't going to pay for a landslide."

That was Kennedy's approach to using humor. He said, "I got into a taxi cab in Chicago at the convention. . . . I thought I ought to tip the cabbie really well and tell him to vote Democratic; then I remembered my daddy; I didn't tip him at all and told him to vote Republican."

That was Kennedy's style. And he could apply that self-deprecating style where it was most appreciated.

Upon receiving an honorary degree at Yale, he quipped: "It might be said that I now have the best of both worlds—a Harvard education and a Yale degree." Can you see how pleasing this was to his Yale audience? How do you think the press responded to Kennedy? They idolized him. Part of it was that ability to laugh at himself. Self-deprecating humor is a tremendous tool for any leader.

Bill Clinton, George W. Bush and Barak Obama learned from Reagan. Today, there are writers who make a good living writing self-deprecating humor for government and corporate leaders. Self-deprecating humor is seen as an essential leadership tool.

When we laugh, we see ourselves in perspective, but we also see ourselves through the lens of kindness and hope. As C.S. Lewis once said, "The ability to laugh at oneself is functionally the closest thing to true repentance." There's something about humor that's very, very close to the grace of God. As William Sloane Coffin once put it, "Take yourself lightly so that like angels, you may fly."

The cardinal rule of humor in the pulpit: if in doubt, don't. Humor is like dynamite. You can use it to blast through a mountain, but it can also blow up in your hands. It can serve you or it can destroy you.

I speak from sad experience. I told a joke one time when I was a young pastor on a man in our congregation. I thought that he and I had a good relationship, and I thought he was the kind of guy who could take a joke. I learned that we did not have that kind of relationship, and I learned, quite painfully, he could not take a joke. And, friend, he was the most powerful man in that church. That's why I'm in publishing today. Well, not completely . . . but you get the idea. So if you have any question about a piece of humor, I would err on the side of caution. If in doubt, don't; it's just not worth the price.

Let me list very quickly some dangers of humor:

Humor can be dangerous if it's inappropriate—and there are no hard and fast rules here. Different people become offended over different things. Pulpit humor must, by necessity, be broad. Irony and sarcasm are the most dangerous forms of humor. People may misunderstand.

Daniel Defoe found that out in a devastating way. It was in the days when the dissenters were persecuted in England. Defoe wrote a satirical pamphlet titled "The Shortest Way with the Dissenters." This pamphlet advocated not repressing the dissenters, but exterminating them altogether. Defoe hoped, by the help of irony, to laugh the persecutors out of court. Do you want to guess what happened? Daniel Defoe had the misfortune to be taken seriously. He heard leading pulpit voices laud his plan for genocide for the dissenters. That's scary!

If it's overused. You're not a comedian. You don't want to get a reputation as a comedian. You're an illustrator and you're simply making your point by using humor.

If it involves put-downs. I'm thinking here of young people in your congregation. I have heard pastors tell jokes about youth styles . . . for example, guys wearing earrings or long hair, etc., and all the adults just cackle. The pastor enjoys telling the joke, but it puts down young people. I look around at some of the young people who are present and I have to ask myself whether any of those young people will ever feel comfortable going to that pastor with a problem. When you use a put-down, it creates a barrier.

I transgressed that barrier not that long ago. I was speaking to a business group. Not able to resist a good joke, I used the line about a young person who had so many piercings "she looked like she fell face-first into a tackle box." Nobody laughed. Then I looked at my audience more closely. Young adults with piercings made up the majority of the group. Oops! [Still learning.]

If it reinforces stereotypes. The reason many pastors (particularly male pastors) may be insensitive to stereotypical humor is that we have never been on the other side. This was brought home to me in a rather direct way by a television program. There was a sitcom years ago, *Flesh and Blood*. It didn't last long. It was about a sophisticated young lawyer in a large Northern city whose brother from back home had moved in with her. He was a stereotypical hick, probably from the mountains of East Tennessee. I say that because her brother was played by actor David Keith who is from Knoxville, my home town. I am a David Keith fan. For one thing, he is an active member of First United Methodist Church of Knoxville.

In this sitcom, however, Keith played a stereotypical Appalachian hick. That part really didn't bother me. We hillbillies have always made fun of ourselves. Remember *Hee-Haw*?

In this show, David Keith had two disgusting children. The boy was particularly obnoxious. He talked in a strong East Tennessee twang and he was an absolute imbecile. *Even worse, his name was King.* Do you get the picture? Here's this gross young fellow, about 13 or 14 years of age and somebody calls to him, "Hey King." Well I've been hearing "Hey King," all my life. But suddenly, I felt my name had been demeaned.

The first time I experienced this, I was on my way to Boston and I thought to myself, "I'm headed to Boston to lead a seminar. Suppose they had just watched *Flesh and Blood* and the only experience they had with somebody from East Tennessee was this awful hick named King. It was absolutely painful to me.

But suddenly, it hit home. For the first time, I knew, at least in a minor way, what it was to be a woman, or to be black, or to be Polish, or to be a member of all the other groups that are the butts of stereotypical humor. I guarantee you that, if you're ever on the other side, you'll make a resolution never to use stereotypical humor again.

Stereotypical humor has no place in the life of a pastor. I'm so thankful for the changes that have taken place in our society. Forty years ago, you could go to a Kiwanis club meeting and somebody would tell a joke that was racist or sexist and folks would laugh. But today, you tell that same story to that same group and people hang their heads in embarrassment, and that speaker won't get invited back. I am so thankful that has taken place. However, we still have a ways to go.

I know, as an old guy, I've had to grow. I got a letter many years ago when we first started having women pastors subscribe to *Dynamic Preaching*. One woman wrote saying, "I'm not a bad driver. Why are you still telling jokes on women drivers?" Before that time, I had never even given any thought to sexist humor. I had to be sensitized, and I was very quickly.

The people whom other folks used for stereotypical jokes in Jesus' time, Jesus made heroes. That's got to be the model for us.

Postscript

There is a battle going on in 99% of the pulpits of America. It is a battle between the preacher's **humanity** and his/her **training**. We were trained to present a message—logical, unified, coherent—that appealed to well-educated, middle-class, middle-aged adults who shared our values. We learned to add credibility to our message by citing authoritative sources. For my generation, it meant quoting men—and yes, they were all men—such as Bonhoeffer and Kierkegaard. And subconsciously, we soaked up a vocabulary befitting our communication style.

Then suddenly, we found ourselves in a new world of communications. Nobody cared any more about authority figures--or logic, unity and coherence, for that matter. Rather than helping our messages to soar, our language set us apart. The theological language we treasured sounded archaic. People were polite: "Good sermon, pastor," but we found ourselves preaching to apathetic and aging congregations. What shall we do? What **shall** we do?

Here's a humble suggestion: Next Sunday, let's leave our carefully polished manuscript in the study. Let's prepare a simple outline based on our text for the day but related to a specific need of the members of our congregation. Let's illustrate each point with a simple, but poignant, story. Let's add a little humor to provide some relief.

And then, rather than looking at our notes, let's look each member in the eye, one at a time, and talk to them person-to-person. In the parlance of basketball, let's go "man-to-man" rather than zone. And let's see if we can't really connect with those precious people who look to us for guidance. We might find that it is far more important to the person in the pew that the person in the pulpit be real than that they be refined.

As Calvin Miller has rightly said, "Most who show up in a service are saying, 'I came here looking for a friend, beginning with you, preacher.'" [56]

St. Paul put it like this: "When I came to you, I did not come with eloquence or human wisdom as I proclaimed to you the testimony about God. For I resolved to know nothing while I was with you except Jesus Christ and him crucified. I came to you in weakness with great fear and trembling. My message and my preaching were not with wise and persuasive words, but with a demonstration of the Spirit's power, so that your faith might not rest on human wisdom, but on God's power" (1 Corinthians 2:1-5).

Go, my friend, and do likewise.

Dynamic Preaching in magazine format is available by calling 1-800-848-5547 or in digital format as part of your subscription to www.Sermons.com.

A beautiful new leather-bound volume of *Dynamic Preaching* is now available. It is a complete 3-year lectionary cycle (approximately 160 sermons). For more details please call 1-800-848-5547.

Shifting Paradigms for Ministry in the 21ˢᵗ Century

Old Paradigms	New Paradigms
Stable, Predictable	Creative Chaos
Quiet Refuge	Center of Excitement
Great Preacher	Effective Communicator
Scholarly, Erudite	Plain Spoken
Cite Authority	Give Modern Example
Theological Abstractions	Concrete Stories
Chaplain	Leader
Clergy Dominated	Empowered Laity
Organ and Choir	Musicians and Performers
Stain-Glass Windows	Fountains (Movement)
Hidden behind Pulpit	Use Body to Communicate
Pastor as Aloof	Pastor as "One of Us"
Auditory	Visual/Kinesthetic
Objective Truth	Subjective Reality
Somber	Have Fun
Position	Personal Influence
Pastor as Star	Pastor as Equipper
Selling	Marketing
Sunday Suit	Casual Friday
Guilt	How to Succeed
Denominational Agent	Entrepreneur

Notes

1. Bruce Larson, *Ask Me To Dance* (Waco: Word Books, 1972), pg. 71.

2. *Overhearing the Gospel* (St. Louis: Chalice Press, 2002), p. 7.

3. *A Place to Dig In* (Nashville: Abingdon Press, 1987), p. 73.

4. Cited in Mark Miller, *Experiential Storytelling: (Re) Discovering Narrative to Communicate God's Message* (emergentYS) (Zondervan/Youth Specialties, 2004).

5. *Ibid.*

6. John Killinger, *Fundamentals of Preaching* (Philadelphia: Fortress, 1985).

7. *The Art of Saying Something.*

8. www.sermoncentral.com/sermons/foolish-or-not-john-bergh-sermon-on–fo ol-156473.asp.

9. I hope I have quoted Dr. Boomershine correctly. I have been unable to find the precise reference for this statement.

10. *The Futurist* (March-April 2012) "A Future of Fewer Words?" Vol. 46.

11. David Buttrick, *Homiletic* (Philadelphia: Fortress Press, 1987).

12. Calvin Miller, *Preaching: The Art of Narrative Exposition* (Grand Rapids: Baker Books, 2006).

13. Thomas J. Peters and Robert H. Waterman, Jr., *In Search of Excellence* (New York: Harper & Row.

14. Cited in Annette Simmons, *The Story Factor: Secrets of Influence from the Art of Storytelling* (New York, Basic Books, 2001).

15. Dallas Seminary Daily Devotional.

16. Alan Jay Lerner (book and lyrics) and Frederick Loewe.

17. Terry Ann Knopf in *Boston Globe* magazine, in *Reader's Digest.*

18. Henry H. Mitchell, *Celebration and Experience in Preaching* (Nashville: Abingdon Press, 1990).

19. Simmons.

20. (Nashville: Abingdon Press, 1990).

21. (Nashville: Abingdon Press, 2012).

22. Eugene L. Lowry, *How To Preach A Parable* (Nashville: Abingdon, 1990).

23. http://www.abpnews.com/news/news_detail.cfm?NEWS_ID=315. Cited at http://www.preaching.com/.

24. John Chancellor & Walter Mears, *The New News Business* (HarperCollins).

25. Henry Grady Davis, *Design for Preaching* (Fortress Press, 1958).

26. Frederick Buechner, *Telling the Truth*, pp. 8–9.

27. (New York: Bantam Books, 1989).

28. Dr. William P. Barker, *Tarbell's Teacher's Manual* (Elgin, IL: David C. Cook Church Ministries, 1994).

29. Bruce Smith, *The History of Little Orphan Annie* (New York, 1982), p. 35. Cited in Loren Baritz, *The Good Life* (New York: Harper & Row, 1982), p. 148.

30. From a sermon by Don Emmitte.

31. *The Cyber Future*, p. 3.

32. I heard Dr. Adams say this on a tape of a workshop he led years ago.

33. *Who Is This Man?: The Unpredictable Impact of the Inescapable Jesus*.

34. Terrie Williams, *The Personal Touch* (New York: Warner Books, 1994).

35. Jeffrey McQuain, *Power Language* (Boston: Houghton Mifflin, 1996).

36. Ron Hoff, *I Can See You Naked* (Kansas City: Andrews and Mcmeel, 1988).

37. James F. Bender, *How to Talk Well* (New York: McGraw-Hill Book Company, Inc., 1949), p. 173.

38. Pat Williams, *The Paradox of Power* (New York: Warner Faith, 2002).

39. New York: McGraw-Hill, Inc., 1993), p. 35.

30. Hoff.

41. Edgar N. Jackson, *How to Preach to People's Needs* (Nashville: Abingdon Press, 1956).

42. Rick Warren, *The Purpose Driven Church* (Grand Rapids: Zondervan, 1995).

43. *1992 Yearbook of American and Canadian Churches* (Abingdon Press, $29.95). Cited in *Cell Church Magazine*, Volume 1, No. 4, p. 4.

44. Jo-Ellen Dimitrius and Mark Mazzarella, *Put Your Best Foot Forward* (New York: Scribner, 2000), p. 28.

45. Roger Ailes, *You Are the Message* (New York: Doubleday/Currency, 1988).

46. Cited SermonCentral Weekly Newsletter, www. Sermoncentral .com.

47. Haddon Robinson, *Biblical Preaching: The Development and Delivery of Expository Messages*, 2nd ed. (Grand Rapids: Baker, 2001), 33.

48. Lawrence Baines in *The Futurist* (March-April 2012).

49. I have misplaced the source of this quote.

50. Lester and Irene David's biography of Senator Robert Kennedy. Cited by Gordon MacDonald, *Forging a Real World Faith* (Nashville: Thomas Nelson, Inc., Publishers, 1989), p. 164.

51. Meadowview Presbyterian Church, Louisville, KY, via PresbyNet, "Eculaugh" one-m#3160, 7/17/96http://www.presbyterianwarren.com/beopend.html. http://www.upcaustin.org/SermonsPubs/Sermons_2006/091006.htmhttp://www.uumcmsu.org/sermons_ folder/sermon 091006.htm.

52. Mark Galli, *Preaching That Connects: Using Techniques of Journalists to Add Impact* (Grand Rapids: Zondervan, 1994).

53. Craddock, *Overhearing the Gospel, p. 79.*

54. Mike Slaughter, *Momentum for Life, Revised Edition: Biblical Practices for Sustaining Physical Health, Personal Integrity, and Strategic Focus.*

55. *Helen Thomas, Thanks for the Memories, Mr. President* (New York: A Lisa Drew Book/Scribner, 2002), pp. 114,115.

56. *Preaching: The Art of Narrative Exposition* (Grand Rapids: Baker Books, 2006).

References

Jay Adams, *A Consumer's Guide to Preaching* (Wheaton, Illinois: Victor Books, 1991).

LeRoy H. Aden and Robert G. Hughes, *Preaching God's Compassion: Comforting Those Who Suffer* (Minneapolis: Augsburg Fortress, 2002).

Elizabeth Achtemeier, *Creative Preaching* (Nashville: Abingdon Press, 1980).

Thomas Boomershine, *Story Journey: An Invitation to the Gospel as Storytelling* (Nashville: Abingdon Press, 1988).

Homer K. Buerlein, *How to Preach More Powerful Sermons* (Philadelphia: The Westminster Press, 1986).

James C. Barry, *Preaching In Today's World* (Nashville: Broadman Press, 1984

John R. Brokhoff, *Preaching the Parables* (Lima, Ohio: C.S.S. Publishing Co., Inc., 1988).

David G. Buttrick, *Preaching Jesus Christ* (Philadelphia: Fortress Press, 1988).

Bryan Chapell, *Using Illustrations to Preach with Power* (Grand Rapids: Zondervan, 1992).

John R. Claypool, *The Preaching Event* (Waco: Word Books, 1980).

Jeff Scott Cook, *Elements of Speechwriting and Public Speaking* (New York: Collier Books, 1991).

Fred Craddock, *As One without Authority* (Enid, Okla.: The Phillips University Press, 1971), p. 52.

John W. Drakeford, *Humor in Preaching* (Grand Rapids: Zondervan Publishing House, 1986).

John L. Dutton, *How to Be an Outstanding Speaker*, 2d rev. ed. (Appleton, WI, Life Skills Publishing Co., 1986).

Clyde E. Fant, *Preaching for Today* (New York: Harper And Row Publishers, 1975).

R. C. Forman, *Public Speaking Made Easy* (New Jersey: Fleming H. Revell Company, 1967).

Harold Freeman, *Variety in Biblical Preaching* (Waco: Word Books, 1987).

Gene R. Hawes, *Speak for Success* (New York: Bantam Books, 1984).

Richard Carl Hoefler, *Creative Preaching and Oral Writing* (Lima, Ohio: C.S.S. Publishing Company, Inc., 1978).

Gloria Hoffman and Pauline Graivier, *Speak the Language of Success* (New York: Berkley Books, 1983).

Michael J. Hostetler, *Introducing the Sermon* (Grand Rapids: Zondervan Publishing House, 1986).

Max D. Isaacson, *Public Speaking & Other Coronary Threats* (Rockville Centre, New York: Farnsworth Publishing Company, Inc., 1984).

Richard A. Jensen, *Telling the Story* (Minneapolis: Augsburg Publishing House, 1980).

John Killinger, *Christ in the Seasons of Ministry* (Waco: Word Books, 1981).

Dennis F. Kinlaw, *Preaching in the Spirit* (Grand Rapids: Francis Asbury Press, 1985).

Charles W. Koller, *Expository Preaching without Notes* (Grand Rapids: Baker Book House, 1962).

Ralph L. Lewis with Gregg Lewis, *Inductive Preaching* (Wheaton, Illinois: Crossway Books, 1983).

Ralph L. Lewis with Gregg Lewis, *Learning To Preach Like Jesus* (Westchester, IL: Crossway Books, 1989).

Sandy Linver, *Speak Easy* (New York, New York: Summit Books, 1978).

Donald Macleod, *The Problem of Preaching* (Philadelphia: Fortress Press, 1987)

Terry Muck, *Liberating the Leader's Prayer Life* (Waco: Word Books, 1985).

Gene Perret, *Using Humor for Effective Business Speaking* (New York, Sterling Publishing Co., Inc. 1989).

John Richters, Jr., *Attacking the Myths of Public Speaking* (Cincinnati: The National Underwriter Company, 1979).

Natalie H. Rogers, *Talk Power: How to Speak without Fear* (New York: Dodd Mead and Company, 1982).

Lloyd M. Perry and Charles Sell, *Speaking To Life's Problems* (Chicago: Moody Press, 1983).

Haddon W. Robinson, *Biblical Preaching* (Grand Rapids: Baker Book House, 1980).

J. Alfred Smith, *Preach On!* (Nashville: Broadman Press, 1984).

William H. Willimon, *Worship as Pastoral Care* (Nashville: Abingdon Press, 1979).

Ralph G. Turnbull, *If I Had Only One Sermon to Preach* (Grand Rapids: Baker Book House, 1966).

Lilyan Wilder, *Professional Speaking* (New York: Simon And Schuster, 1986).

Ronald L. Willingham, *How to Speak So People Will Listen* (Waco: Word Books, Publishers, 1968).

Made in the USA
Columbia, SC
29 July 2019